S 4
∧ 4
81 ↄ

Places of interest

See Information pages
for further details

1 Pennine Way
2 Upper Teesdale, Durham
3 Hutton Roof, Cumbria
4 Southerscales Scar, Yorks.
5 Humphrey Head, Lancs.
6 Malham, Yorks.
7 Great Ormes Head, Caernarvon
8 Derby Dales
9 Ouse Washes, Cambs.
10 Barnack Hills and Holes, Cambs.
11 Devil's Ditch, Cambs.
12 Therfield Heath, Herts.
13 Dunstable Down, Beds.
14 Gower Peninsula, Glamorgan
15 Upper Thames valley meadows
16 Aston Rowant, Oxfordshire

17 Grangelands and Pulpit Hill, Bucks.
18 Brean Down, Somerset.
19 Cheddar Gorge, Somerset
20 Somerset Levels
21 Berry Head, Devon
22 Dorset Coast Path
23 Hod and Hambledown Hill, Dorset
24 Fyfield Down, Wiltshire
25 Salisbury Plain, Wiltshire
26 Avebury, Wiltshire
27 Chiselbury Camp, Wiltshire
28 Danebury Hill, Hants
29 Queen Elizabeth Country Park, Hants.
30 Old Winchester Hill, Hants.
31 North Downs Way
32 Box Hill, Surrey

33 Kingley Vale, Sussex
34 Arun Valley, Sussex
35 Ditchling Beacon, Sussex
36 South Downs Way
37 Cuckmere Valley, Sussex
38 Seven Sisters, Sussex
39 Queendown Warren, Kent
40 Wye and Crundle Downs, Kent
41 Burren, County Clare

Discovering the Countryside with David Bellamy

Grassland Walks

Country Code

Whenever and wherever you are out walking, please follow these simple rules:

- Guard against risk of fire
- Close all gates behind you, especially those at cattle grids, etc.
- Keep dogs under control
- Keep to paths across farmland – you have no right of way over surrounding land
- Avoid damaging fences, hedges and walls
- Leave no litter – take it away with you
- Safeguard water supplies
- Protect wildlife, plants and trees – do not pick flowers, leave them for others to enjoy
- Drive carefully on country roads
- Respect the life of the countryside – and you will be welcomed.

Discovering
the
Countryside
with
David
Bellamy

COUNTRY LIFE BOOKS

Grassland Walks

Acknowledgements
Line-drawings by Kenneth Oliver

Additional photographs pages 36–37 Cambridge University Photography

The Publisher and David Bellamy would like to thank the following organisations for their help in preparing this book:
Royal Society for Nature Conservation
Nature Conservancy Council
Northamptonshire Naturalists' Trust
Hampshire and Isle of Wight Naturalists' Trust

In particular we would like to express our gratitude to the gallant team of experts, Frank Perring, David Streeter, Paul Toynton, Trevor Elkington and Francis Rose, whose hospitality, enthusiasm and vast knowledge of the countryside is only hinted at in these pages.

Published by Country Life Books
an imprint of Newnes Books
84–88, The Centre, Feltham, Middlesex, TW13 4BH, England
and distributed for them by
The Hamlyn Publishing Group Limited
Rushden, Northants, England

© 1983 Newnes Books, a Division of The Hamlyn Publishing Group Limited

First published 1983

ISBN 0 600 35637 X
Printed in Italy

Photography by Peter Loughran

Foreword

Every time you get out the lawnmower you are conducting an ecological experiment, as you are not only doing battle with nature but are also aiding and abetting members of the most successful plant family in the world: the grasses. You don't believe me? Well, just stop mowing the lawn for a few years and see what happens. It will become more and more difficult to see anything in your garden as the lawn is taken over by shrubs, bushes and, eventually, turns into woodland.

Every year you put an enormous amount of energy into keeping your lawn nice and short by holding back the process of natural selection which, without you, would replace the open lawn with trees. In so doing, you are helping the grasses and certain other herbs to maintain their very successful stake in the environment. In the absence of people and mowers, grassland are maintained in their natural state by at least four other agencies: climate, soil, grazing animals and fire. Climate, especially too little rain, and soil, especially too much drainage, can so stunt and limit the growth of shrubs and trees that a natural grassland will develop. Fire and grazing can help in the maintenance of such grassland,

Contents

prairie or savannah, in much the same way as your lawn mower, by removing anything which is more substantial than a blade of grass. It is here that the grasses and grass-like plants, as well as certain other types of plants, come into their own as they are able to survive this constant grazing. They produce in effect, a self-generating cafeteria for a variety of grazing animals and an open plant community in which many other sun-loving plants can thrive.

The vast bulk of the British grasslands are not natural as they have been created and are maintained by man either with animal husbandry or more recently with leisure pastimes and sport, in mind. Nevertheless, many are very ancient and offer some of the most diverse and beautiful floras and faunas to be found anywhere in Britain. One of the most interesting questions is, where did all these beautiful grassland plants occur before man came on the densely wooded British scene? The answer is here amongst these pages and in the many grassland walks, which are often amongst the most rewarding of all. Grasslands are also nice places to take a picnic, but, when you do, be careful where you sit and always remember to take your rubbish home and leave all the grassland flowers for other walkers to enjoy.

Bellamy's wild grass chase

Wherever you stand in the British Isles you are not too far away from grass. Yes, even in the middle of the vast acreages of moorland, there are grasses forming an important part of the living community. So, I thought I wouldn't move too far from my home, or off the tarmac and simply take a trip from the coast to the top of the Pennines and see what grasses I could find. The journey produced many kinds of grasslands, each one with its own old favourite species and each one with its surprises. What have sheep's fescue, common bent and daisies in common? Grazeability, and, from the look on the sheep's and cattle's faces, palatability! But they also have trample tolerance; a factor which is of immense importance when faced with a herd of hungry animals. The flowering heads of the grasses were there all the way along my journey, blowing in the breeze and repeatedly reminding me of their dominance in the landscape. I wonder what the same journey would have been like before man and his domestic animals nibbled their way onto the scene?

Here I am up in the Pennines amidst a glorious scene full of grasses (with a splash of colour from some knapweeds!) Over the wall is a small flock of sheep which work pretty hard at making sure it stays that way, for without their incessant grazing it would soon return to scrub and woodland.

Information

Grasses

The flowering plants contain many exciting families, such as the wierd and exotic orchids or the composites with their unique flower-heads (capitula) consisting of mini-flowers, but the grass family – Gramineae – must be the most successful of them all. There are approximately 620 genera containing over 10,000 species which can be found all over the world from the tundra wastes to the tropical rainforests. Over large areas of the globe they form the main feature of the landscape, such as the African savannah lands and the South American pampas. The structure, which allows them to put on continued growth despite being eaten back, means that many species of animal depend on them as a prime source of food. Included in this category must come man, for, although we do not eat the leaves of grasses in the way of sheep or cattle, the grain of certain species forms man's staple diet in many countries. It is said that half the world's population subsist wholly or partly on one grass – rice, *Oryza*. The land for the production of cereal crops such as wheat *(Triticum)* and barley *(Hordeum)* covers vast areas of the Earth's surface. In the tropics the plantations of sugar cane *(Saccharum)* are an important part of the economy satisfying not only man's sweet tooth but also helping to provide some of his energy needs. Bamboo, which can grow to a height of thirty metres within a few months, is one of the principal building materials of the Third World.

In the British landscape grasses are cultivated or maintained as the prime food source for our livestock or as a cereal crop. In this book we are mainly concerned with the rich grassy swards that cover so much of our landscape tended and kept by centuries of grazing. It must be remembered that even the apparently natural scene of the grassy slopes of the Yorkshire Dales is man-made, as all these areas are below the natural tree-line and, before the advent of man, would have originally been covered in forest.

For many people, even our common grasses are, at first glance, too similar to tell apart but with a little practice these important members of our plant communities will become familiar and more easy to identify. And, although there are as many as 150 native grasses, the vast majority of the land is covered by a small group of very common species, listed opposite.

Structure of a grass

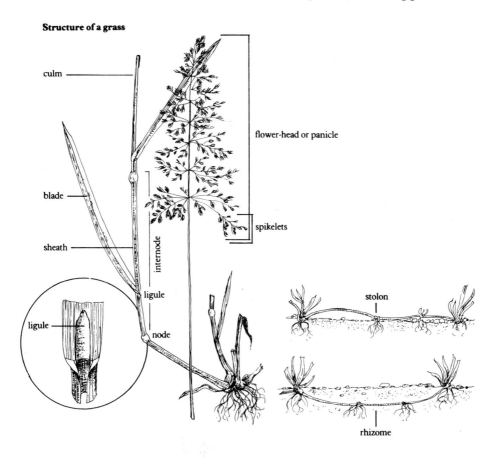

culm

blade

sheath

flower-head or panicle

spikelets

internode

ligule

node

ligule

stolon

rhizome

Twenty common open grass species

perennial rye-grass *Lolium perenne*
timothy grass *Phleum pratense*
false oat-grass *Arrhenatherum elatius*
cocksfoot *Dactylis glomerata*
Yorkshire fog *Holcus lanatus*
smooth meadow-grass *Poa pratensis*
quaking grass *Briza media*
sweet vernal grass *Anthoxanthum odoratum*
sheep's fescue *Festuca ovina*
red fescue *Festuca rubra*

mat grass *Nardus stricta*
crested dog's tail *Cynosurus cristatus*
fine bent grass *Agrostis tenuis*
upright brome grass *Zerna erecta*
common wild oat *Avena fatua*
couch grass *Agropyron repens*
tufted hair grass *Deschampsia ceaspitosa*
meadow fescue *Festuca pratensis*
rough meadow-grass *Poa trivialis*
meadow foxtail *Alopecurus pratensis*

Chalk and limestone in the British Isles

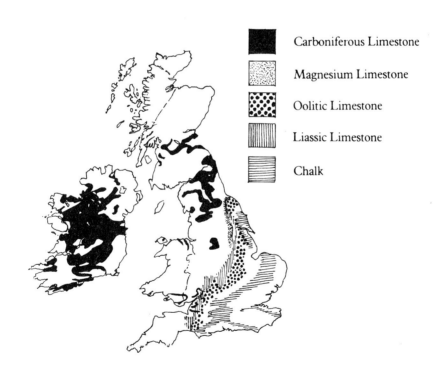

■ Carboniferous Limestone

▨ Magnesium Limestone

▨ Oolitic Limestone

▥ Liassic Limestone

▤ Chalk

Although people generally refer to chalk and limestone as if they were different types of rock, chalk is, in fact, a very pure form of limestone, which is rock that has over fifty per cent calcium carbonate. Indeed, the Upper Chalk is, in places, 98 per cent pure calcium carbonate. As a general rule, chalk is a softer rock than limestone, hence, the undulating rounded hills of the Downs which contrast markedly with the massive rocky outcrops of the Carboniferous Limestones of the Yorkshire Dales. An important band of Oolitic Limestone stretches in a great arc from the south west up to Yorkshire. Although this has not produced the impressive landscape features of the other limestones, it is none the less important where exposures occur.

Bellamy's wild grass chase

It is true to say that wherever you go in Britain you are never far away from that most important family of flowering plants – the grasses. To show you just how important grasslands are as part of the landscape I've decided to go on a series of walks today in the north-east of England, starting right down on the beach near Teeside and finishing up on the very tops of the Pennine hills.

So here I am with my feet almost in the sea and the very first plant that I have found growing on the beach is a grass – lyme grass, to be exact, *Elymus arenarius*. Now this is a nice, big grass, so it gives me an ideal opportunity to show you the very special features of grass plants. First of all, beneath the surface all the plants have a root system and this one is doing an important job binding the sand together. Then above the surface we have the stem or, to give it its correct botanical name, the culm. This stem is divided into a series of hollow sections called inter-nodes which are joined by nodes – the joints that stick out on your bamboo canes. The wierd thing about the stems of grasses is that you can't actually see them. This is because they are covered by a sheath of leaves. It is from the nodes that the leaves first arise; they then run up the stem enveloping it in a sheath until suddenly they turn away to form the leaf blade. On this lyme grass it is a beautiful blue-green colour. At the junction where it turns outwards, if you take a close look, you will see a thin membrane-like growth on the inside of the leaf called a ligule. In this grass it is just a tiny rim of tissue but in some other grasses it is much bigger. Also if you look carefully you can see two rather wierd lobes at the base of the leaf blade; these are called auricles. These features are always worth finding as they often help to identify the type of grass you have. If we continue to look up the stem we can see another node, another leaf sheath and blade, followed by another node and so on, until we see the culm sticking out of the top with a great mass of flowers on it.

Within this basic structure grasses have adapted to cope with a whole range of environmental problems. Here we are on a sandy beach which is a great place to visit on a sunny day but it is a pretty tough place for a plant to live. They can't make use of the seawater so they have to take advantage of any rainwater that falls. The rain then sinks away into the sand very quickly or is evaporated away by the salty winds. So our grass has to be able to hold on to what water it can

get. If you look at the leaf of the lyme grass and run your fingers across its surface you will notice that it is ridged and furrowed. Down in the deep furrows are the stomata pores from which water is lost and these are almost roofed over with a weft of microscopic hairs to cut back on the loss. If the going gets really tough the leaf will roll up into a tube and protect itself almost entirely. So that's our first grass – now let's start heading inland and see what we can find.

Behind us is a series of sand dunes which owe their existence almost entirely to the marvellous binding properties of the root systems of another grass – Marram grass, *Ammophila arenaria*. Beyond that is a low cliff where we should find more members of the grass family.

A short, sharp climb has taken us onto the edge of the cliff and here I am sitting looking out to sea from a nice patch of grassland sward. If I get down and have a closer look at it, the first thing that I can see is that the dominant plant is, you've guessed it, a grass. But what sort of grass? Well, here's the culm and there's a long, long leaf which is setaceous or hair-like. That tells me that I'm looking at red fescue, *Festuca rubra*. Really

Right Down at the seaside! Here is one of the first intrepid colonisers of the sands – *Elymus arenarius*, lyme grass. It has tough leaves that can roll up to stop it losing moisture and protect it from enthusiastic botanists.

Opposite Up on the cliff top there is already a dense covering of grasses. Here we have the fine leaves of red fescue, *Festuca rubra* and the striking flowers of the bloody crane's-bill, *Geranium sanguineum*, which is a good indication of rich limestone grassland. The name crane's-bill refers to the fruits which look like the beak of a miniature crane.

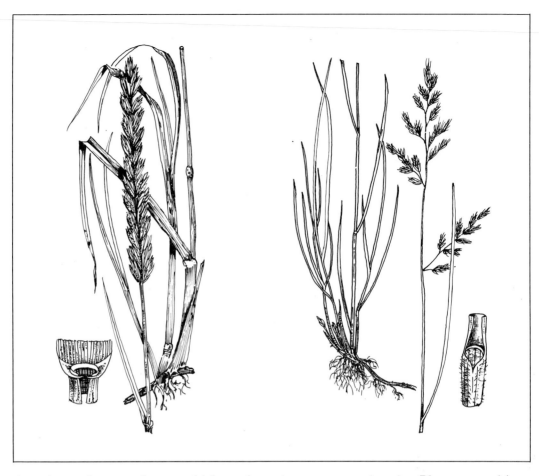

the only way for you to be sure which species of grass you have is to look very closely and make some drawings of the important parts like the leaf shape and the ligule and compare it with a good guide when you get home. A must for anyone keen to study grasses is a wonderful book with lots of clear drawings, called simply, *Grasses*, by Charles Hubbard. Once you know what to look for and are familiar with the common species it is not nearly so difficult as it first appears. Start by trying to identify some local grasses.

In amongst the red fescue are an awful lot of other plants and standing out above everything else are the striking deep red flowers of the bloody crane's-bill, *Geranium sanguineum*. Now, because it is a lime-loving plant that immediately tells me that the underlying rock here, as we are in the North East, is magnesium limestone. If we search around we should find some other plants that like a fairly basic soil. Yes, there is some lovely rock-rose, *Helianthemum chamaecistus*, with its yellow crinkly petals, and over here is some salad burnet, *Poterium sanguisorba*, both plants that you wouldn't be surprised to find along any stretch of the chalk slopes of the southern Downs. Here is something that tells me we are still close to

the sea – sea plantain, *Plantago maritima*. The leaves of this plant grow in a typical plantain-like rosette, but are rather fleshy and channelled and every now and then, along the edge, there is a little glandular tooth which says that it is sea plantain rather than the much commoner long-leaved ribwort plantain, *P. lanceolata*. So we can see that a grassy sward can allow room for plenty of other plants to grow. However, normally if the grassland was left to its own devices it would eventually be taken over by coarser plants and scrub-up, climaxing as an area of woodland. In a way the grasses sign their own death warrants by producing such a super matrix for other plants to grow in. But this little scrap of grassland right on the coast is rather special in that the constant effects of high winds and salty sprays have kept the ranker plants at bay. Therefore this is an example of truly natural grassland and would have been the type of place where plants which now cover our open countryside first originated. Almost everywhere else that you see grassland it has been created and maintained directly or indirectly by man. Every time you get out your lawn mower and mow the lawn you are holding back the process of natural succession to woodland.

When man first arrived on the British scene he found that nearly all the landscape through which he had to travel was festooned, swathed and covered in forest. The only places where there were open habitats that could support grasses in any numbers were mountain tops, sand dunes, the edges of saltmarshes, maybe the occasional river cliff and sea cliffs like this. But why do the grasses appear to thrive under all this constant cutting and chewing to which man and beast subject it. Well, we can see the answer to this if we just look at the leaf of our red fescue. There's the leaf blade again and below it is the sheath and there right at the base is where the growth of the leaf actually occurs, from what is known as a meristem, where cells are actively dividing to provide new growth. So if I was a cow and came along chewing at these delicious grasses I could eat my fill and still leave the meristem right there at the bottom, so that the grass could still thrive. So where there is this grazing pressure only the plants that can do this or that have regenerative buds right down on the surface, or even underneath the ground, can survive. So the grasses are at an enormous advantage. Another way in which grasses are able to make full use of these open situations is that they can spread vegetatively, putting out numerous underground stems called rhizomes or surface ones called stolons which can soon make a dense green carpet of grasses, as anyone who has planted a lawn will know.

Talking of lawns, if we just clamber over this ridge we can have a quick look at some superbly kept areas of grassland. Here I am standing beside an immaculately maintained green on a golf course. We've just made sure that we aren't disturbing anyone, so if I get right down on my tummy I can have a close look at this mini-habitat. Absolutely perfect! This patch has been so beautifully tended and clipped that it is difficult to make out what type of grasses are growing. There appears to be three different sorts here and then nothing else at all, which just shows what man can do, for the patch we have just walked over from, not ten metres away, has been recently surveyed and contains over 100 species of flowering plant.

Now, as we go on our journey we are going to see how man has managed certain areas of the countryside, often with the result of creating large areas of grassland. So if we head for the car we will drive along and see what we can find.

Well, here we are only a few miles inland and I am standing by a major road looking at a very different landscape from the cliffs and sand dunes we have just left behind. I can see a whole variety of man-made grasslands. This is what I like to call lowland eutrophic farmland. Eutrophic means nutrient-rich, and here there are enough potential nutrients to support lush grasses, hedgerows and even the odd bit of woodland. If I just scan the view I can see pastureland with sheep grazing. There the colour of the grass appears as a dull greeny brown. And then I can see a lot of improved pastures which are a much brighter green. In the foreground many of the fields have cereals growing in them. Remember that cereals are grasses as well. In this part of the country the farmers will be growing wheat, oats or barley. At the moment the crop is turning a rich golden

This young golfer looks as though he has just failed to hole his putt. I wonder if he knows how many species of grass his ball has just rolled over, for although it looks as uniform as a a well-hoovered carpet, as every gardener will tell you, the best lawns and greens will have a mix of grasses to give them strength as well as compactness. A popular combination includes common bent, Chewings fescue and red fescue.

A lovely splash of yellow by the roadside provided by a thriving colony of birds-foot trefoil, *Lotus corniculatus*.

colour and will soon be ready for harvesting. Behind these fields the farmers have already done this and the soil has been freshly ploughed ready to be sown with winter wheat. So everywhere we look, there is a patchwork of man-made grassland held together by hedgerows. The dominant standard tree in these and the small patches of woodland is the ash, *Fraxinus excelsior*. Ash is a kind tree to grasses as it is late in coming into leaf and then it has these delicate compound leaves which allow a lot of light down to the soil.

Right now we have this marvellous view over Wierdale with Durham Cathedral in the distance. But when man first arrived here it would have looked very different. In fact, he probably would not have had a view at all as there would have been a dense canopy of forest. Today there is this marvellous diversity of habitats and, indeed, it was the prosperity that came with the clearance of the forest and the development of lowland agriculture that contributed to the wealth of the society which built the Cathedral.

We've now jumped back in the car and driven just a little further inland. I've stopped off here to take a look at a very underrated type of grassland – the roadside verge. Along this stretch it has been regularly cut up to about three metres from the tarmac. Because it has been mown we should be able to find quite a diversity of plants growing

Opposite **A classic view of lowland agriculture with a rich mixture of arable and grazing land. Notice the tall hedgerows and stands of trees, all of which indicate the richness of the land.**

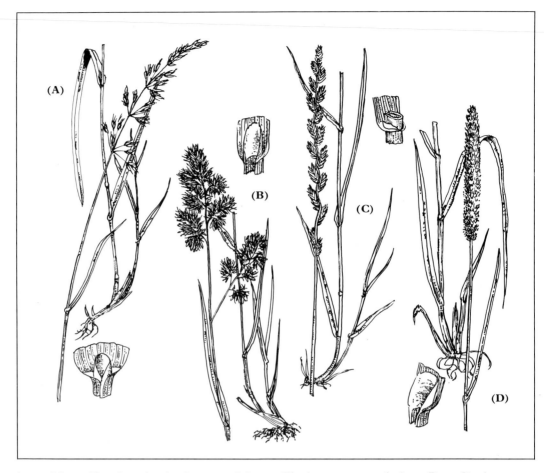

here. Now, I've just knelt down and immediately I can see some white clover, *Trifolium repens*, and the good old dandelion, *Taraxacum officinale*. Dandelions are one of those plants that has regenerative buds right down in the middle of the rosette of leaves. So that when the council workers come along with their mower or when you are mowing your lawn the blades go over the top of the bud and new leaves can start to grow. There are, of course, many grasses here and if we look over by the hedge, where the council mower has failed to reach, we can see if we can identify some of them.

Here we have the 'big four' grasses of our roadsides. The first one that I can pick out is the false oat-grass, *Arrhenatherum elatius*, which is big in more than one sense of the word as it is almost as tall as half a Bellamy. Now to confirm my identification I need to look somewhat closer at the grass. Here's a leaf blade and there is the sheath, so if we look at the junction we should find the ligule and, yes, there it is; a very short one, probably no more than a millimetre in length. To do the job properly you should make a careful sketch and measure it.

Now, the next grass is much, much easier to identify because its flowering panicles look

like its name – cocksfoot, *Dactylis glomerata*. The lower branches of flowers stick out at an angle that is supposed to resemble the spur on the foot of a cockerel. Again, this can be quite a tall grass; up to 140 centimetres high. If you look at the ligule you will notice that it is longer than the previous one; usually between two and ten millimetres in length with a ragged pointed tip. Cocksfoot is a good drought-resistant grass as it roots deeply and is able to tap supplies of water throughout the year.

Over here is a very important grass perennial rye-grass, *Lolium perenne*. The farmers use it a lot as it provides highly nutritious grazing for long periods of time. It has a very distinctive flowering spike with the tufts of flowers arranged alternately on either side of the stem to give it a rather nice flat appearance. The ligule on this plant is very short, like the oat-grass, but if you look closely you will see that it does have these two lobes or auricles coming off at the base of the leaf blade.

If I look around a bit I might find the fourth of our big four grasses. Now here it is. A very distinctive grass called timothy, *Phleum pratense*. This is a nice soft grass that used to grow wild in water meadows. It is

named after an American agriculturalist called Timothy Hanson, who recognised its worth back in the early eighteenth century and introduced it to the United States. It doesn't do too well as a pasture grass but is very important as a fodder crop. You can spot it by its narrow, cylindrical spike of flowers, which give it its other name of cat's-tail. The ligule is blunt and usually up to six millimetres long.

All these grasses flourish in these rich eutrophic lowlands, as do the farmers' crops. And just over the hedgerow here we can see a field of stubble; all that remains after the farmer has harvested and bailed up his cereal crop. Perhaps the farmer will burn the remains or just leave it to rot and plough it in later in the year. But the important thing to notice is that the flora of the field is completely man-managed. Except for a narrow band just by the hedge there is very, very little there that the farmer has not deliberately put in. He has used all sorts of selective herbicides, insecticides and fungicides to ensure that. So between the road and the field this little strip of verge and hedgerow represents a vital linear nature reserve that is covered with grassland. Just to make the point about how interesting these verges can

Top **A combined harvester cutting the corn. The threshed corn is held in a large storage tank whilst the straw is thrown out at the rear. The crop here is probably a strain of barley,** *Hordeum*, **which, of course, is a grass.**

Bottom **Amidst a sea of intensive arable farming the hedge-banks and roadsides are the only areas left where nature can have its sway. Here we have a tall sow-thistle,** *Sonchus*, **framing a field of cereals.**

Blue moor-grass, *Sesleria caerula,* **with its blue head of flowers and boat-shaped leaves.**

be, if we walk along here I will show you a plant that has an interesting story to tell.

Now, here I am standing on a fairly steep embankment alongside the road and just in front of me is an area that has only a sparse covering of vegetation. It has been kept this way probably by a combination of council mowing and accidental burning. The underlying rock is the magnesium limestone that we met down on the coast and just here I can see a rather special plant – the lovely pink and red flowering spikes of sainfoin, *Onobrychis viciifolia.* When you go on your holidays in the Mediterranean you'll find it growing in the grassland and roadsides there. It follows the limestones and chalks all the way from the sunny south through Britain to here. And that's as far as it goes. It doesn't even grow on the other side of the road. It seems as if the joint influences of soil and climate allow it to grow this far and no further. There are several other plants in this area that reach their northern limit on these magnesium limestones around Durham. But the special point of bringing you here is that if this little corner of the roadside verge became overgrown with bushes and trees, then this plant would not be able to survive and this little part of the country near Durham would not be quite as special as it is. So when you are out on your walks don't dismiss the miles of verge and look straight over the hedge. You never know what you might be missing.

Right, let's get back in the car and I'll take you to a little piece of nearby grassland and show you a species of grass that really tells you that you're 'up north'.

We've just parked the car and taken a short walk to another rather special place and all around me is a superb open grass community on magnesium limestone. Nearly every bit of this special type of grassland is under threat either from industry, who have quarried vast areas of it to make such things as fire bricks to line the great steel furnaces, or from farmers who quite logically see more profit out of ploughing it to grow crops or reseeding it. But, although there are many very rare and unusual plants here, today I want to show you a grass that before I came to the North East I'd never seen – the blue moor grass, *Sesleria caerulea.* It is one of the first grasses to come into flower in the spring and in April and May you can always tell it by its wonderful shiny blue head of flowers. During the rest of the year you can see these beautiful leaves. They have a duck-egg blue colour on the inside, rather like the lyme

grass we saw earlier on. If you look more closely they have quite distinct veins like tram-lines running along the middle. The leaf is keeled with a distinct boat-shaped tip. This grass is common up in the high arctic, and right the way across the limestones of Scandinavia. You will even find it on the tops of the limestone mountains of the Dolomites and the Alps. In fact, it might be classed as an arctic-alpine plant. So what is it doing growing down here in the middle of lowland County Durham? Well, we're not quite sure. But we do know that it grows especially well on the magnesium limestone. So this is one unique piece of semi-natural grassland – I say 'semi' because obviously without the intervention of man it wouldn't be here at all, but I am afraid the further efforts of man to manipulate his environment means that its days are numbered.

We must now move on out of these lowlands and see what grasslands we can discover further up the road.

Right **A flowering spike of sainfoin,** *Onobrychis viciifolia,* **photographed at its most northerly outpost in Britain, a roadside verge near Durham.**

Opposite top **A very ancient form of grassland management – a deer park, which is currently playing host to a considerable number of sheep!**

Opposite bottom **A beautiful view across a patchwork of fields in the Dales. Although the grasses in the valleys are still doing very well, the presence of dry stone walls indicates that the environment is harsher.**

We are now quite a bit further inland and have just pulled off to look at one of my favourite spots in the area. It is a very old form of grassland management. If we look around we will probably see some clues as to what this is. Look, there's a lovely area of grass which looks as though it is fairly regularly grazed. There are magnificent trees dotted all around and a castle in the background. But if you look at the trees you can see that they have all been browsed up to a particular height which almost certainly reflects the reach of the animals. If you start looking about you can see some rather elegant animals grazing quietly in the distance. They are fallow and red deer and, of course, this is a deer park. During the medieval times deer parks were considered important hunting and pleasure grounds for the elite of the age and many of the parks we have today are directly descended from those times. So that is another type of grassland to add to our list.

Further along now and here is another good place to stop at – the village green. Today they are used as a place to walk the dog or just sit and maybe watch a game of cricket. In the past, however, they were a place of vital importance. It was to the village green that the local livestock was taken when danger loomed in the guise of predators or outside raiders. However, we'll just sit down and have our sandwiches and see how the local cricket team is faring. Not too well, I'm afraid to say. They might get a few more runs if the out-field wasn't so slow. But that is because our friends the grasses are growing so well. I can see some cocksfoot, perennial rye-grass and a new species, meadow foxtail, *Alopecurus pratensis*.

Its now later in the day and we are further inland and I can actually see the tops of the Pennines in the distance. It is a very different landscape. Gone are the lush hedgerows with all their lovely shrubs. Their place has been taken by dry-stone walls, which make a much more effective barrier than a very, very slow-growing hedge. If you look around, many of the trees, unless they are growing in sheltered hollows, are pretty stunted. This is because we are now getting into a much harsher environment than down in the lowlands. Still, everywhere you look there are fields. In fact, I can remember seeing a wonderful British Rail poster when I was a little boy which said: 'Come to the Dales'. It was illustrated with a picture showing a patchwork quilt of different coloured greens picked out by dry-stone walls. I honestly thought such a beautiful man-made landscape as that could not exist. But there it is; a patchwork quilt.

Each one of the fields full of grass is a gigantic solar cell fixing energy from the sun's rays and doing an immense job for the farmer in feeding his livestock. Up here the climate is too harsh to grow arable crops. However, many centuries ago the climate was warmer and you can often find signs of the old lynchets formed by the ploughs of medieval farmers. Nowadays there are only cattle and sheep here.

Let's have a look and see what grasses we have growing in the area. If we start by looking again at the roadside verge I can see the same sorts of grasses that we found lower down but they are not growing quite so tall. There's a typical mixture of false oat-grass, rye-grass and cocksfoot with some Yorkshire fog, *Holcus lanatus*. No, I'm not describing the weather, that's the name of a rather

gorgeous hairy grass. I like to think that it got that name as it holds the morning mist that creeps along the hillside just above the surface. Next to it is another *Holcus* grass, creeping soft grass, *H. mollis*. They are easy to tell apart because the creeping soft grass has a little tuft of hairs on each of its nobbly nodes, rather like an ageing boy scout's knees. These two grasses become more and more important in the verges and pastures as we gain altitude. If we look over the wall we can see a very different type of grass community. The tall grasses have gone and we have a short cropped mixture of sheep's fescue grass *Festuca ovina*, and the highly adaptable red fescue. In amongst these, in full autumn fruit, are the distinctive flowering spikes of crested dog's-tail, *Cynosurus cristatus*. If you look at the spike you will immediately notice that one side is flat and the other has dense tufts of flowers. A good way of remembering the shape is to think of a

It is very important that the farmer achieves the correct stocking rates for his fields as the quality of the grass will soon deteriorate if he has this at too high a level. From the contented look on this cow, I would think that her farmer is doing a good job.

dog that lives in a house and which continually bangs its tail on the floor until one side is almost perfectly flat whilst the other is bushy. I'm sure you've met one. Well, there it is: the crested dog's-tail. This grass is an indicator of acid grassland, so not the best soil but certainly good enough to keep the grass going.

If you look at the sheep droppings in the field you can see where they have been grazing. Sheep are very fastidious grazers and will keep going back to eat the sweeter tasting grasses. So after a time they can begin to change the make-up of the grass community in the field. As long as the farmer is careful and doesn't stock his fields with too many sheep no damage will be done and the grasses will continue to thrive. There are a few patches of stinging nettles, *Urtica dioica*, in the field. Now, I will tell you how they got to grow there. I can't see any cows in the field at the moment but they are certainly around

as there is a whacking great cow-pat right down in front of us. If I were to lift it up I would find that the grasses beneath it had all gone yellow because all the light had been shut out. It will take quite a long time for that cow-pat to be broken down and during that time it will be releasing phosphorus and other nutrients into the soil. Now, stinging nettles are great phosphorphiles and will readily take advantage of such a situation, crowding out the grasses.

If I just cross over the road I can show you a very different type of grassy field. Here the farmer has decided to do something radically different. He has ploughed the field and reseeded with a mixture of plants. It is a much lusher green than the more traditional pasture we have been looking at. Unfortunately it is not in flower but I would guess that it contains some special strains of perennial rye-grass with a little timothy grass. In amongst the grasses I can also see

some white clover which would have been planted with the grass as its roots help fix the nitrogen in the soil, providing a very cheap source of nitrogen fertiliser. It is called a short-term ley and is very green compared with the other side of the road. Mind you, to achieve this the farmer will have had to expend a lot more energy. He has had to plough it and seed it and fertilise it to get it established and will have to continue to ply it with herbicides and fertilisers to maintain its productivity. A difficult choice for the farmer.

Up here the climate is very harsh in the winter and so the sheep have to have their feed supplement during these bleak months. In order to do this the most productive areas

Above **The evening light catching the flowering head of one of our most common grasses, cocksfoot,** *Dactylis glomeratus.*

Left **Here we are right up in the Pennines. As you can see the trees have almost all gone and these summer pastures will be covered in snow for large parts of the winter.**

are often set aside not as pastures for grazing but as fields where the grasses are allowed to grow as a crop and are then cut in the summer for hay. They then become meadows and some of the meadows in this part of the world have very ancient histories.

Now we've driven a bit further along to one of these meadows and the first thing that I hope we are going to notice is the incredible diversity of the plant species growing in them. There is an interesting length of stone wall separating the roadside verge from the meadow. If we take a look, unlike our pasture and the ley, we should find that there is not too much difference between the two sides. Both do seem to have most of their plants in common. I can see quite a list: meadow foxtail, oxe-eye daisy, *Chrysanthemum leucanthemum*, tufted vetch, *Vicia cracca*, wood vetch, *V. sylvatica*, field scabious, *Knautia arvensis*, knapweed, *Centaurea nigra*. Absolutely super. And over there are some more – the melancholy thistle, *Cirsium hetrophyllum*, with its distinctive nodding head. Then there's wood crane's-bill, *Geranium sylvaticum*, lady's mantle, *Alchemilla vulgaris*, and some great burnet, *Sanguisorba officinalis* in the damper bits. The list is long which reflects partly the continuity of management over the centuries and the fact that neither the verge or the meadow are grazed but are sown at regular times of the year, which allows for a greater diversity of plants. Most of these meadow plants set their seed fairly early in the year so that the mowing doesn't cut short their life cycle. You will have probably noticed the words wood and *sylvaticum* popping up in my list. This is because some species that are considered as woodland plants in the south of England crop up here as meadow plants. All together these northern hay meadows are certainly to be treasured. It would be unforgivable if we let them completely disappear.

Still, we still have to travel a bit further if we are to reach the tops of the Pennines before the end of the day so it's back to the car.

Now we are quite high up, well over the 400 metre mark, and the landscape is starting to look decidedly different. Yes, it's moorland with patches of grassland coming right up to the edge of the road. A deep ditch beside the road to carry the water away warns us that it is a very rainy environment. The trouble with so much rain is that not only does it water the grasses but it also leaches the soils so that they will tend to be very acid and poor in nutrients. Naturally the grasses tell us that.

The sheep's fescue is still with us but here it is a rather scruffy plant. There are also some new ones. This is sweet vernal grass, *Anthoxanthum odoratum*. It is one of the easiest plants to remember. It has a fresh yellow-green colour and has a dense spike of flowers. Now, hold the spike of flowers and give it a sharp tug – usually you find that the flower-bearing culm parts company with the rest of the plant. All you do now is chew the base of your stalk and you should find that it has a lovely sweet taste. That is how it got its name and the taste is in fact coumarin, a chemical which gives hay its distinctive sweet smell. It is also said to stimulate the appetite.

The grasses up here don't grow well enough to provide hay for the sheep in winter and so when the farmer takes his sheep in during the colder months he has to bring up hay from the lower areas. In fact, many of these fells are 'stinted', which means that they can only hold a certain number of sheep each year. When most of the rules of upland grassland management are adhered to, the grasses remain as a nice tasty mixture and both the farmer and the sheep stay happy. But I'm afraid over-grazing in some areas has started to alter things quite dramatically. As we have said, sheep are fastidious eaters and will select the lusher grasses to eat and leave the tougher, harsher ones. So these unpalatable species have an enormous advantage and begin to slowly but surely take over the grassland community. Here is one of the toughest grasses of the lot – mat grass, *Nardus stricta*. Again it is an easy grass to identify with its one-sided comb of spikelets and its bristle-like tufts of leaves. I'm going to chew some of it. Ugh, horrible, stringy stuff. No wonder the sheep give it a miss. Here it is covering the ground, so the sheep are pretty hard pressed to find a tasty meal. In places you can see where they appear to have pulled it up and almost thrown it down again in disgust. A sure sign of over-grazing.

There is another type of plant up here that the sheep don't like, which takes advantage of the over-grazed land. That is heath rush, *Juncus squarrosus*. It grows in almost circular tufts with a central flowering stalk, that may be as much as twenty centimetres high, sticking out of the top. It is a tough old plant but it is ideal during the winter months for the grouse that come along and eat the seeds when all else is covered with snow.

So here we are up in the Pennines and wherever we have stopped on our journey up

The last outpost! Above this point you are in open moorland but even here the grasses, such as mat grass, *Nardus stricta*, are dominant.

from the coast we have met members of the grasses. Right up here we also have some other members of the graminoids, the grass-like plants. We have just looked at a rush and here is a sedge. This is carnation sedge, *Carex panicea*, which has these greyish leaves that look like those of the carnations you grow in your garden. Sedges are easily told from grasses as they have a three-sided flowering stem.

Before I head back home to write up my field notes of the day, all I am going to ask you to do is to think of the importance of grasses in this world of ours. They provide an absolutely perfect cover for the soil, holding it against erosion, and protecting it from the wind and rain. They form a self-regenerating salad for the animals that come along to eat them. In many countries they provide the staple food, whether it is rice or wheat for bread. If they are allowed to grow in their own natural way they provide a special habitat for a whole variety of other plants which don't like being over-shadowed. They are tolerant of all types of uses, from having games of football played on them to providing a mini-forest for all kinds of invertebrates. All plants are import-ant but in my opinion the grasses are the most important of them all.

A limestone grassland walk

Once upon a time, not all that long ago, someone said, 'Let's map the flora of the British Isles on the basis of the ten kilometre grid square, so making a detailed inventory of Britain's vascular plants and their distribution'. A fantastic idea and a mind-boggling amount of data, but Britain's botanists took up the challenge and tramped the fields, moors, forests and hedgerows to accomplish just that. Frank Perring took on the task of collecting and collating the data and producing the maps. Undaunted, and with all that data at his fingertips, he went on to the even more exacting job of General Secretary of the Royal Society for Nature Conservation, the body which helps to look after both that floristic heritage and the fauna which it feeds and protects. Who better then, to lead us into the delights of the 'Hills and Holes' of Barnack. A fantastically important reserve for many of the dots on Frank Perring's maps and one which was saved only in the nick of time from the inexorable process of plant succession, by members of the Northamptonshire Naturalists' Trust and the Nature Conservancy Council.

A view out across the 'Hills and Holes' of Barnack in spring with a Hawthorn, *Crataegus monogyna* **in full blossom in the foreground.**

Information

Chalk and limestone grasslands

The chalk and limestone grasslands of Britain, particularly the Downs of Southern England, are perhaps one of the most invigorating landscapes to explore for the walker. Their wide open vistas provide splendid views of the surrounding countryside and their gentle contours mean that they are easy on the feet. An added bonus is that these dry hills and coombes only really come to life during sunny summer days – so the nicer the weather during your walk, the more you are likely to see.

Plants

One of the chief attractions of these grassy swards is the profusion of wild flowers. Many of these flowers are found growing only on calcareous soils and not on more acid soils; these are called calcicoles (Latin *calx*: chalk; *colo*: inhabit). They can therefore be used as an indicator for chalky or limestone soils. The following is a list of some of the more widespread calcicoles:

hairy violet *Viola hirta*
chalk milkwort *Polygala calcarea*
horse-shoe vetch *Hippocrepis comosa*
kidney vetch *Anthyllis vulneraria*
dropwort *Filipendula vulgaris*
salad burnet *Poterium sanguisorba*
common rockrose *Helianthemum chamaecistus*
autumn gentian *Gentianella amarella*
yellow-wort *Blackstonia perfoliata*
fairy flax *Linum catharticum*
squinancywort *Asperula cynanchica*
travellers' joy *Clematis vitalba*
clustered bellflower *Campanula glomerata*
hoary plantain *Plantago media*
small scabious *Scabiosa columbaria*
stemless thistle *Cirsium acaulon*
carline thistle *Carlina vulgaris*
bee orchid *Ophrys apifera*
fragrant orchid *Gymnadenia conopsea*
pyramidal orchid *Anacamptis pyramidalis*

Invertebrates

Calcareous habitats are equally as rich for invertebrates as they are for plants and are particularly renowned for their butterflies. The following list is a selection of species to look out for:

meadow grasshopper
    Chorthippus parallelus
common field grasshopper
    Chorthippus brunneus
common green grasshopper
    Omocestus viridulus
striped-winged grasshopper
    Stenobothrus lineatus
six-spot burnet moth *Zygaena filipendulae*
small blue butterfly *Cupido minimus*
chalkhill blue butterfly *Lysandra coridon*
adonis blue butterfly *Lysandra bellargus*
common blue butterfly *Polyommatus icarus*
brown argus butterfly *Aricia agestis*
marbled white butterfly *Melanargia galathea*
meadow brown butterfly *Maniola jurtina*
small heath butterfly *Coenonympha pamphilus*
grizzled skipper butterfly *Pyrgus malvae*
dingy skipper butterfly *Erynnis tages*
small skipper butterfly *Thymelicus sylvestris*
large skipper butterfly *Ochlodes venata*
meadow ant *Lasius flavus*
glow worm *Lampyris noctiluca*
bloody-nosed beetle *Timarcha tenebricosa*
heath snail *Helicella itala*
striped snail *Cernuella virgata*
wrinkled snail *Candidula intersecta*
Kentish snail *Monacha cantiana*

Sites

North Downs Way Long-distance footpath forming part of the ancient Pilgrims' Way from Winchester to Canterbury and passing through some lovely chalk downland scenery. Read The North Down Way (HMSO) for further details.
South Downs Way This long distance footpath from Beachy Head in East Sussex to the Hampshire border passes through some of the best areas of this splendid stretch of Downs. Read the South Downs Way by Seán Jennett (HMSO) for further details.

Box Hill, Surrey. This beauty spot in the North Downs is a very popular area for weekend walking and despite its summer crowds of picnickers it still has a rich chalk flora and fauna which can be discovered by those prepared to explore. Juniper Hall Field Centre nearby offers courses on the natural history of the area. National Trust.

Old Winchester Hill, Hampshire. This chalk hill at the west end of the South Downs, is another popular weekend beauty spot. It has many interesting chalk plants including orchids and the round-headed rampion. National Nature Reserve.

Queen Elizabeth Country Park, Hampshire. This park at the west end of the South Downs includes Butser Hill which has steep grazed hillsides. An Iron Age demonstration farm is a feature of the park.

Danebury Hill, Hampshire. A hill in the Hampshire Downs with a hill-fort dating back to the Bronze Age. Good chalk flora. Nature trail.

Kingley Vale, West Sussex. This area of chalk downland and wood has some lovely open areas as well as an ancient yew forest. There is an Iron Age fort and tumuli. Nature trail throughout the year. National Nature Reserve.

Ditchling Beacon, East Sussex. One of the higher parts of the South Downs with diverse scrub and chalk grassland flora and fauna. National Trust and Sussex Trust for Nature Conservation reserve.

Seven Sisters, East Sussex. This famous beauty spot at the east end of the South Downs includes the chalk cliffs of Beachy Head. Country Park area including downland walks and meadowland in the Cuckmere Valley.

Wye and Crundle Downs, Kent. One of the richest areas of the North Downs for chalk plants including many orchids and butterflies. Area includes a spectacular chalk coombe called the Devil's Kneading Trough. Nature trail. National Nature Reserve.

Queendown Warren, Kent. An area of old chalk downland with a rich flora and fauna, including orchids and butterflies. Leaflet. Reserve managed by the Kent Trust for Nature Conservation.

Dorset Coast Path. This is the Dorset section of the huge south-west Peninsula Coast Path. The section between Lulworth Cove and Ringstead Bay takes in some magnificent chalk cliffs and downs, including Durdle Dor.

Hod and Hambledown Hill, Dorset. A high chalk hill in the Dorset Downs crowned by an Iron Age hill fort. Excellent chalk flora and fauna.

Salisbury Plain, Wiltshire. This area has some of the most extensive areas of chalk grassland in Britain. Unfortunately, a great deal is MoD land and access is limited to a few days in the year, such as Bank Holidays. Porton Down has excellent chalk flora.

Avebury, Wiltshire. There are more prehistoric monuments in this area than anywhere else in Britain. The famous Avebury rings encompass the village. Nearby is West Kennet Long Barrow, a huge Neolithic burial mound. Also superb downland scenery.

Chiselbury, Wiltshire. An ancient hill fort near Salisbury on an ancient routeway which now forms a 'green road' from Salisbury to near Shaftesbury.

Fyfield Down, Wiltshire. Large area of chalk down with public access along footpaths. Good chalk flora and fauna. National Nature Reserve.

Brean Down, Somerset. A narrow Carboniferous Limestone headland at the edge of the Mendips near Weston-super-Mare. Rich flora especially on the south-facing slopes.

Black Rock, Cheddar Gorge, Somerset. A reserve including the steep valleys sides of the Gorge and some of the Mendip plateau. Good Carboniferous Limestone flora, including woolly thistle and many butterflies. Nature trail. Leased by the Somerset Trust for Nature Conservation.

Berry Head, Devon. A Devonian Limestone headland in Torbay. Many rare and interesting plants. Nature trails and splendid views.

Gower Peninsula, West Glamorgan. There are an excellent series of walks that can be taken from the village of Rhosili to explore the Carboniferous Limestone scenery of this beautiful peninsula. Best visited in early spring for such flowers as spring cinquefoil and vernal squill.

Aston Rowant, Oxfordshire. A large reserve on the Chiltern Scarp, split by the M40 motorway. Rich in chalk flowers and butterflies. Nature trail on Beacon Hill. National Nature Reserve.

Therfield Heath, Hertfordshire. Despite its name this Chiltern reserve is outstanding for its chalk flora and fauna which includes the pasqueflower and the chalk-hill blue butterfly. Managed by the Herts. and Middlesex Trust for Nature Conservation in agreement with the owners.

Grangelands and Pulpit Hill, Buckinghamshire. A chalk downland reserve in the heart of the Chilterns, including a fine range of chalk flowers and butterflies including the small blue and marbled white. Managed by the Berks, Bucks and Oxon Naturalists' Trust.

Dunstable Downs, Bedfordshire. An area south west of Luton which is at the edge of the Chilterns. Ivinghoe Beacon (National Trust) is 244 metres high and provides good views of the Chilterns. Whipsnade Zoo is nearby. Totternhoe Knolls is a local reserve managed by the Beds and Hunts Naturalists' Trust.

Devils Ditch, Cambridgeshire. A spectacular linear earthwork dating from about 500 A.D. stretching for over seven miles. The rich chalk grassland on the ditch is managed by the Cambridgeshire and Isle of Ely Naturalists' Trust.

Barnack Hills and Holes, Cambridgeshire. A superb area of Oolitic Limestone grassland in the Soke of Peterborough, overlaying the remains of a medieval quarry. National Nature Reserve with smaller area managed by Northamptonshire Naturalists' Trust. See overleaf.

The imposing Church of St John the Baptist with its ancient Anglo-Saxon tower made of Barnack Rag from the quarry on the outskirts of the village. The spire is a more recent addition.

Spring in the countryside should be a magical time. This is when even the most hardened city dweller looks to the budding trees and hedgerows and promises himself that he must get out more often. Yet in these days of intensive arable farming he frequently finds that the countryside is not as he remembers it – the pastures with their carpets of spring flowers are difficult to find. Many of the old footpaths are still there but they flank great fields of winter wheat and barley where the only obvious signs of wildlife are the skylarks singing high in the sky. In May we went for a walk in a little piece of old England where the larks were singing above a very different landscape – open country, yes, but an intriguing landscape of mounds and gullies, hummocks and hollows, almost like a golf course without the fairways. This was Barnack Hills and Holes, a unique place with a superb limestone flora overlaying the remains of a once thriving medieval quarry. These disused quarries often provide excellent places for discovering plants and the diversity of flowers at this site has been known for a long time. Our guide for the day was the well-known botanist Dr Frank Perring, who left his busy job as General Secretary of the Royal Society for Nature Conservation to show us around one of his favourite reserves.

We started our walk actually in the churchyard of the village of Barnack itself. Whilst we studied the features of the imposing tower Frank told us a little of the history of the church and its connection with the quarry.

'Here we are at Barnack, which is one of the villages in the Soke (ancient administrative area) of Peterborough. In some ways you can consider this district as part of the Northamptonshire extension of the Cotswolds. The common feature of these areas is the band of oolitic limestone which runs in a great arc from south west England up to the Humber. It is this rock that has been quarried to provide the distinctive building stone that typifies so many buildings throughout the region. The limestone here at Barnack is probably the best building stone in the whole of the inferior oolite, partly because of its very durable qualities.

'We are standing at the foot of the impressive tower of the Church of St John the Baptist which dates from 1020. It is one of the best remaining Anglo-Saxon towers in Britain. You can still see the details on the exterior stone. The tower has vertical stone ribs that even today retain their sharp edges. If we look more closely at the stone itself we can see that this ragstone, as it is called, has an enormous amount of shelly material in it. Some other types of oolite have egg-shaped shell fossils in them which give the rock its name (Greek *oion*: egg). We have fairly clear evidence that this stone was first quarried here in Roman times. In the Norman period, when the great abbeys and cathedrals of the Fens were built, this stone, particularly the Barnack Rag, was used a great deal. There are some very fine examples of stonework in

Barnack Rag in Ely Cathedral and Peterborough Cathedral – the Norman part of which was built from Barnack stone – and many abbeys such as Ramsey, Crowland, Thorney and Bury St Edmunds. These abbeys were granted rights to quarry the ragstone and there are records that show that in one case the monks of Ramsey provided their brethren at Peterborough with four thousand eels annually as rent for the stone. An indication as to when the Barnack Rag began to run out can be found by looking at some of the colleges at Cambridge. By studying, for example, Corpus Christii it is quite clear that after the mid-fifteenth century they were going elsewhere for their stone. If you look around the church here there is further evidence of this, as none of the monuments to the deceased worthies are made of Barnack Rag after this time.

'The position of Barnack was an important factor in the success of the quarry as the River Nene is only about four miles to the south and the River Welland two miles to the north. So after a short land journey, probably by ox-cart, the stone could be easily transported by barge.'

The church tower, appropriately enough for the start of a nature trail, had what looked like a cockerel and some vine leaves still clearly showing in relief against the warm-coloured limestone. Below this there was a round-headed Norman window with two more birds on either side of its apex. It was strange to think that they had been impassively watching the changing scene for almost an entire millenium.

We then moved on through the village to the quarry itself – Barnack Hills and Holes Nature Reserve. At the edge of the reserve the hawthorn scrub was alive with the songs of birds. Willow warblers and chaffinches were in full voice and as we looked out across the reserve the brilliant yellow of a cock yellowhammer flashed by. We strolled out towards the centre and after finding a 'hill' that gave a good view of the site we asked Frank to tell us some more about the history of the quarry.

'Looking around you can imagine how this place must have looked when it was abandoned in the middle of the fifteenth century. You can see all about us are these hills and holes. The holes are where men with picks and shovels would have quarried the stone and the humps or hills are the spoil heaps which were simply left by the workings. Although it was quarried for approximately

1500 years it would have been done very gradually – not in the way that they are able to excavate whole areas today. This was important as it meant that the original vegetation would have been able to slowly recolonise the quarry as one area became worked out and a new area was exploited. Also the vegetation around the quarry would have helped in providing wind blown seeds. Doubtless animals from neighbouring land would have got in and carried seeds in as well. Today, if we look across to the west away from the village, all we can see is arable farmland. However, in the fifteenth century all this area would have been dry limestone grassland. So, as the quarries were abandoned they were surrounded by suitable plants ready to recolonise the bare soil. The reason that this particular spot has never been converted to arable land is quite simple: the hills and holes make it almost impossible to plough. It has, therefore, been left more or

A detail of the tower showing a cockerel standing above a column of vine leaves. Notice how sharply the relief still stands out, despite almost a thousand years of erosion.

less undisturbed for over five centuries.

'At some stage in the history of the site when the area around it began to be cultivated, a stone wall was erected around the disused quarry. This remained there right up until the First World War when it was dismantled and used for road building. Until then the wall was a vital factor as it meant that sheep could be grazed on the turf without straying onto the surrounding crops. Even when the practice of sheep grazing died out, the rabbits would have helped to keep the grass short. Also, being in close proximity to the village meant that fairly frequent fires were lit which no doubt helped to keep the scrub at bay. All this was important in maintaining the original species composition of the site, for if it had been left to its own devices it would soon have scrubbed up and lost its rich diversity of herbs.

'In the early 1950s the introduction of myxomatosis meant that the rabbits were wiped out and the wooded area to the south-east of the site began to encroach. If you had come here three or four years ago you would have been standing in a wood of Turkey oaks. If nothing had been done, the whole area would have been under woodland shade. Moreover, once the rabbit grazing stopped two dominant grasses moved in – tor grass *Brachypodium pinnatum* and upright brome *Bromus erectus*. Both these species come in when grazing stops and the tor grass, in particular, seems to be encouraged by burning. All this was clearly detrimental to the very exciting low growing plants which were characteristic of the original grassland. In 1965 the Northamptonshire Trust for Nature Conservation decided they ought to do something about it and acquired, by agreement with the Burghley Estate Trust, management of the south-west quarter of the area. This was fenced off partly to mark the boundary of the reserve and partly so that sheep grazing might be reinstituted. However, it has only been the last few winters that there have been sheep here, since 1976 when the Nature Conservancy Council declared the whole site of fifty-five acres a National Nature Reserve and fenced it further. Today the majority of the site is cleared of scrub and regularly grazed.'

Having talked about the history and management of the reserve we were keen to look at some of the plants and so we headed further into the miniature rolling landscape in search of spring flowers. We were soon rewarded with a view of perhaps one of the

Two aerial photographs of Barnack showing the effect of the removal of grazing pressure on the vegetation of the 'Hills and Holes'. The top photograph was taken in July 1948 and it can be seen that, apart from a few areas of scrub in the far left of the picture, the site was largely open grassland. Up until this time a combination of sheep and more recently rabbit grazing had helped to keep the scrub out. In the photograph below, taken in late June 1976, the encroachment of scrub, mostly Turkey Oak, from the wood was quite extensive. The more open area in the top left of the picture had been kept clear by the local Trust. Today, with fencing and the reintroduction of sheep grazing, as well as physical clearance of the scrub, the reserve has become more open again.

The beautiful deep purples of two blooms of the pasque flower, *Pulsatilla vulgaris*, a rare plant of old limestone and chalk pastures.

most easily recognised of flowers of calcereous grassland – the cowslip *Primula veris*. The distinctive nodding heads of yellow flowers were growing in profusion on the steep slopes of the hills. These plants still grow abundantly where the conditions are favourable but unfortunately in large areas of lowland Britain they are now much more scarce than they used to be. They are often to be found on hedgebanks and field edges where they have escaped the plough or the herbicides and fertilizers that the farmer has applied to improve his grassland. If you find them growing across a field it can sometimes indicate that the farmer is still using traditional methods of management and it is worth exploring for other interesting grassland flowers.

Further exploration was certainly rewarded here as we soon came upon a rather special flower – the pasque flower, *Pulsatilla vulgaris*. The bell-shaped flowers were a beautiful rich purple colour, contrasting with their yellow anthers. We asked Frank to tell us some more about these striking flowers.

'If we had really wanted to see the pasque flowers at their best we naturally should have come at Easter. However, although these are meant to be Easter flowers they have a fairly long flowering season. I have seen them as early as the middle of March and here we are towards the end of May and there are still some with new flowers. Here we have a nice mixture of flowers at various stages. There is one that has probably just opened – its flowerhead is pointing upwards and it will stay like that for about 48 hours and then droop. One over there is just closing up which means it will soon droop down. Whilst they are pointing upwards, interestingly, they are capable of movement. The one that has just opened could well close tonight and then open again tomorrow. If it clouds over

Top **A classic plant of grasslands and old pasture – the cowslip,** *Primula veris*. **This plant still adds a lovely touch of spring colour to hedgebanks and fields where more traditional farming methods are still used.**

Left **A late afternoon view of the 'Hills and Holes' showing the extraordinary contours of the site. The 'holes' are the areas that were dug out to remove the limestone and the 'hills' are simply the spoil heaps left by the working.**

The elongated stems and silky plumes of a group of pasque flowers, *Pulsatilla vulgaris,* **silhouetted against the sky.**

and rains that could also make it close. The leaves are finely divided like a mayweed or yarrow, which can mean that the plant is easily missed when it is not in flower. After flowering, the stem elongates and the seed head, with its silky plumes, dominates the plant. Oddly, although around here the plants are obviously producing seeds, people who have studied these plants in detail have found that seedlings rarely establish themselves in the wild. So this plant survives vegetatively in old turf and even if it doesn't flower it can survive by producing these very fine leaves. If a site is ploughed up or destroyed that is the end of it, and we have seen the pasque flower disappear gradually in

this country through the centuries. A couple of hundred years ago there were probably eighty sites in Britain for this plant but now the figure is down to about thirty.

'This flower underlines the importance of careful management on old limestone pastures like this. When the NCC declared this area as a National Nature Reserve there were about a thousand separate flowering rosettes here. In the last six years or so the numbers have gone up to about ten thousand as a direct result of the reintroduction of controlled sheep grazing.

'They are one of the most beautiful wild flowers we have and obviously people come here to see them. However, we always say

Centre **The flower-heads of Horseshoe vetch,** *Hippocrepis comosa,* **arranged in attractive whorls of yellow flowers. This plant, which only grows in profusion in short calcareous or limestone grassland, is the food plant of the caterpillars of both the chalkhill blue and adonis blue butterfly,** *Lysandra coridon* **and** *L. bellargus.*

Left **A close-up of the flowering spike of the man orchid,** *Aceras anthropophorum.* **Only those at the bottom of the spike are fully open, showing the extraordinary 'helmeted' lip shaped like a human figure.**

that although they may appear abundant here, they should not be picked as they are such a rare plant nationally.

'Another unusual plant which shows the advantages of management is the man orchid, *Aceras anthropophorum.* This again is a plant of lime-rich pastures which is at the northern edge of its distribution here. Before the sheep grazing there were approximately a thousand flowering spikes; now it is calculated that there are around eight thousand or more. So we have swung from having a site with a progressively denser cover of Turkey oaks and rank grass to this rich open grassland community. If we have a closer look at this bank we can see just how rich it is.

'Here are some man orchids that are just starting to flower – they always remind me of a little man in armour whose visor has slipped. Later on in the year there will be other types of orchid flowering, such as the pyramidal orchid, *Anacamptis pyramidalis.* However, it is the sheer diversity of species that is the most impressive feature of these old grasslands. The total number of species within just this 55 acre reserve is almost 250, which is pretty high. You also get a high number of species within a very small space – if you were to count the species in a metre square you could easily find over thirty.

'A fascinating aspect of this site from an ecological point of view is that it is very good

Above **The crinkly yellow flowers of the common rock-rose,** *Helianthemum chamaecistus*, **a typical plant of dry sunny slopes. It can form a dense mat of flowers where conditions are favourable.**

Above right **A fine specimen of the hairy rock-cress,** *Arabis hirsuta*, **a member of the cabbage family of plants.**

Right **Purple milk-vetch,** *Astragulus danicus*. **This plant has an interesting eastern distribution following the limestone grasslands up into Northumberland and the calcareous dunes of Scotland.**

A male common blue butterfly, *Polyommatus icarus*, **feeding on a composite. This is the most widespread and common of the 'blues' and can be found in a variety of habitats.**

for studying the micro-distribution of plants within a small area. If you walk around these humps and hollows you can easily move from a north facing slope to a south or west facing one and find that you have a complete change in the plant composition. If we have a look around I will show you what I mean.'

We wandered across a stretch of the reserve to an area with many steep slopes, and from the crest of one of the 'hills' Frank showed us some of the variations in these mini-downs.

'Here we have a steep south facing bank and if we just walk down it one of the things we notice is that there is quite a lot of bare earth which is becoming covered with a lovely crop of horse-shoe vetch, *Hippocrepis comosa*. This plant has about six or seven pea-like flowers in a clustered head and when they produce fruit the pods consist of little segments, each of which looks like a little horseshoe. This is a species which is often associated with dry south or south-west facing slopes. There are some pasque flowers

here which also tend to be found on warm south and south-west facing slopes. Another species which favours this aspect is the salad burnet, which is a member of the rose family and is wind pollinated, often becoming dominant in these lime-rich communities. Other plants that do well on these more open areas are the dwarf "shrubs" of limestone grassland such as the common rock-rose, *Helianthemum chamaecistus*, which has creeping woody shoots and can form dense mats where conditions are favourable. It has these beautiful yellow flowers with rather crinkly petals. Thyme is another dwarf shrub which is very successful here. The main grass species of the short turf here is sheep's fescue *Festuca ovina*, which has these very fine needle-like leaves.

'Just over the crest of the hill, on the north facing slope, you notice that there are a great number of cowslips and, more importantly, the sward is much denser with hardly any bare patches at all: there is not only a thick covering of upright brome but also the tor

Another tiny plant of open turf communities – the common milkwort, *Polygala vulgaris*. Although minute, when looked at closely, these plants can be seen to have intricate flower structures.

it is found in northern and eastern Britain, following the limestone up into Northumberland, and into the Scottish calcereous dunes. So, in a sense, it looks out across the North Sea to Denmark. It does not go very far south on the chalk, and is found only just south of the Thames, rather like the pasque flower. It has this typical tight head of purple flowers with rather hairy leaves made up of many leaflets.

'Here is another herb which is covered in hairs – this is *Arabis hirsuta*, hairy rock-cress. It is a small member of the cabbage family or Cruciferae, a name which is derived from their typical four-petalled flowers, which on some species could be said to resemble a cross. This particular plant has a little rosette of basal leaves and a tall flower spike that has leaves clasping the stem with these little white flowers at the tip. Again it is a plant of dry lime-rich slopes with plenty of open space.

'Across here is another little plant of these open turf communities – common milkwort, *Polygala vulgaris*, which has curious little flowers with great blue sepals on either side. They are very like fumitories, which can occur as a common garden weed.

'An important point to remember is that having looked at all these plants we should expect to see some of the diversity of insect species that live on them. Unfortunately it is a bit blustery today – but down amongst these hollows out of the wind we should come across the common blue butterfly, *Polyommatus icarus*. The caterpillars of this little butterfly feed on the birds-foot trefoil. The reserve here also has some rarer species that will be flying later in the year and on a hot June day the reserve is positively throbbing with butterflies.

'The trouble is that in the summer it also throbs with people. It has always been a site that has been near people. People and the Hills and Holes go together – after all, the landscape is largely created by man. And this area is still regarded as a recreation area by the villagers of Barnack. People walk their dogs here and it is a wonderful place for children to play. Up to a point that is an advantage in that the open nature of the place after grazing stopped was maintained to an extent by the villagers trampling and lighting fires, etc. But today we have also to contend with a vastly expanding population in Peterborough and in an area of intensive arable farming like this there are not that many "open spaces".

grass. Because of the dominance of these grasses it is difficult for small low-growing herbs to survive and although there is some birds-foot trefoil, the horse-shoe vetch and pasque flowers are absent. A complete contrast to the other bank and all within four or five metres.'

We made our way over some more of the hills, noticing the constantly changing pattern of flowers and grasses, until we arrived at another south facing slope which was flecked with purple. This time it wasn't the pasque flowers but a leguminous plant. As we knelt down to have a closer look Frank described the plant to us.

'This is a patch of purple milk-vetch, *Astragalus danicus*. There are two more species of *Astragalus* in Britain, one of which is found in the Scottish mountains. This one has the specific name of *danicus* which indicates that it is also found in Denmark. It has an interesting distribution in that

'These slopes are wonderful places for sliding down but that is obviously detrimental to the quality of the site. You could lose large areas of pasque flowers and other flowers if that was allowed to go on. Where erosion is causing a problem we have cordoned the area off by simply posting out an area and linking it with coloured string. The sign says it all – Nature Conservancy Council Plant Protection and Erosion Control – Please avoid the area. It is a way of pointing out to people that you cannot go on using a place excessively without destroying the very thing for which it has been set aside. What we have to do is achieve a balance. People causing a problem are approached and talked to very kindly and usually if it is explained for example, why it would be better if they moved their picnic to a less sensitive area, they become quite interested in the flowers and readily accept the point. There are bound to be some problems but

that is better than totally excluding people. However, some control is necessary. One only has to go to Box Hill in Surrey on a summer weekend to see what twenty thousand pairs of feet regularly tramping up there can do to the plants. In many places the turf, which was once as rich as anywhere, has been reduced to daisies and plantains, as they are the only species that can resist that amount of pressure. One has to be aware of these facts. Abusing a site like this by trampling out the pasque flowers is really rather like scratching your name on Westminster Abbey.'

Certainly Frank had shown us a display of spring flowers that would be hard to forget – the obvious delight that other visitors were experiencing at seeing the rich colours of the plants was plain to see. As we drove back down the A1, the relentless uniformity of the verges and the surrounding fields only served to underline the importance of reserves like Barnack Hills and Holes.

If you are very patient you might be lucky enough to see one of Britain's few species of reptiles, the common lizard, *Lacerta viridis.* **This handsome creature is soaking up the sun amongst some of Barnack's famous limestone.**

45

A downland walk in mid-summer

An afternoon out in the field with David Streeter is always a memorable experience, but when it is on his home ground and with chalk downland to boot, it becomes a real occasion. Why is it that the thin nutrient poor soils overlying the chalk are so rich in plants and insects? The answers lie, in part, in these pages and in your own experiences when walking the downs, as most great natural historians including Charles Darwin himself have done before you. I still find it fascinating to think that within a few miles of the great metropolis of London, it is possible to see almost everything which fired Darwin's imagination to ask searching questions about the inter-relationships between flowers and their insect pollinators, some of which have never been satisfactorily answered to this day. The answers to these questions are there amongst all that staggering diversity and beauty waiting to be discovered. Perhaps you could be the one to find them.

A superb view of a stretch of the South Downs in East Sussex. The absence of surface water and the almost treeless, smooth skyline is typical of the Downs. The hillside in the foreground is studded with anthills, a feature which usually indicates that the grassland is very old.

A downland walk in mid-summer
with
David Streeter

Southern England might not be said to have the dramatic scenery of some areas of Northern Britain but on a balmy summer's day, a walk across a stretch of the rolling Downs is certainly an exhilarating experience by any standards. The chalk hills of the South Downs exhibit some of the most archetypal of British landscapes and have long been considered as splendid walking country. Indeed, apart from the numerous public footpaths and open spaces there is an official 80-mile (129 kilometres) long-distance footpath that runs along the ridge of the South Downs from near Eastbourne to Petersfield in Hampshire and in places follows a route probably used as far back as Neolithic times. These whale-backed Downs have also been a favourite haunt of naturalists for centuries. The reason for this is the tremendous variety of plants and animals that can be found there, as well as, one suspects, the very beautiful landscape itself.

We drove south one bright day in July to visit an area where the traditional farming practices were still being employed in order to find out what has attracted people to this part of the world for so many years. And who better to be our guide than David Streeter, well-known broadcaster and Reader in Ecology at Sussex University, which is itself in the heart of the Downs?

There was hardly a cloud in the sky when we stepped out onto one of David's favourite stretches of the Downs. Our first stopping point was to be a slope a short walk away so we struck out across the gentle contours of the hills and valleys. All around us insects were busily moving from flower to flower. A whitethroat suddenly flew up from a nearby patch of scrub and burst into a babble of song before gliding down to disappear once again. Butterflies were patrolling the grassy sward on either side of us. On a distant slope we could see a loose flock of sheep unhurriedly working their way along the hillside, their outlines shimmering in the afternoon heat. Already we were eager for David to tell us more about the richness of the area. So, having found a suitable vantage point, we sat down to soak in the atmosphere and allow David to unfold some of the history of this beautiful scenery.

'We are sitting on a nice, warm south-facing slope of a dry valley in the chalk countryside of the South Downs in East Sussex. The other side of the valley is covered with short grazed grassland and some cereal crops. Out to our left is a beautiful slope covered with a flock of sheep, not something that one sees so often on the chalk of the South Downs these days. The heyday of sheep-grazing on these hills was in the middle of the last century and lasted right up until the First World War. Since then there has been a progressive decline in the area of old downland turf which is being grazed in the traditional manner, and a reciprocal increase in the amount of arable farming. But today we have come to one of the finest remaining pieces. It is managed as a nature reserve, and is being grazed on a basis which is very similar to the original farm management practised over a hundred years ago. The traditional image of the South Downs as sheep-grazing country is due largely to one particular animal: the Southdown sheep. In 1761 a farmer called John Ellman, whose family farmed at Hartfield in the north of Sussex, moved with his father from the Sussex Weald to the countryside around Glynde, just to the east of Lewes. There he set about improving the rather scruffy-looking sheep with speckled faces that he found grazing the chalk. He eventually produced what became the most famous of all breeds of sheep, the Southdown, which ultimately contributed to all the other Downland breeds: the Hampshire, the Dorset, the Oxford and so on. Now, sadly, the Southdown flocks are very much reduced because the carcass is rather small for modern-day needs. The sheep that we can see here today are larger cross-bred animals.

'Looking at this countryside from a natural history point of view, the exciting feature is the wealth of flowers and insects. And the most astonishing aspect of this, which is not always immediately apparent, is the number of different wild flowers that can be found. Just here is should be possible to find no less than twenty-five species of flowering plant within a square foot or about forty species per square metre. I would think that must hold the record as the richest of all plant communities anywhere in western Europe. There are very few places where you can see that number of different species in such a small area. It is claimed that the plants of some alpine zones and sand-dune habitats can be as rich but somehow I doubt it.

'Why is it that the flora of these chalk downs is so extraordinarily rich? The first thing to consider is the rock which underlies the soil – chalk. If we pick up a lump of chalk we can see that it is pure white. In fact, it consists of almost nothing but pure calcium

The rich plant communities of the downland slopes have developed in conjunction with hundreds of years of sheep grazing. The constant nibbling of the sheep has kept the tiny plants low and prevented coarser grasses and scrub from encroaching. Sadly, this type of scene is now on the decline and vast areas have been turned over to cereal production as can be seen on the hill top opposite.

Above **Together with the sheep, rabbits have traditionally been responsible for keeping the grassy swards of the Downs closely cropped.**

Right **A dew-covered inflorescence of the round-headed rampion,** *Phyteuma tenerum.* **This beautiful plant is restricted to dry chalk slopes in southern England.**

Far right **The tall flowering spike of a fragrant orchid,** *Gymnadenia conopsea,* **one of the more frequent downland orchids.**

Above **Although the common twayblade,** *Listera ovata*, **does not have the showy flowers of its cousins, its complex flowering structure gives it away as a member of the orchid family.**

Left **Pyramidal orchid,** *Anacamptis pyramidalis*, **showing the typical dome-shaped flowering spike and the deeply lobed lower lip of the flower. This orchid is more widespread than most but it is only commonly encountered on the southern calcareous grasslands.**

carbonate. This means that when it weathers to form the soil there is nothing in it that can contribute to the nutrients of the soil other than calcium. So the soil will have little potassium or phosphorous as well as virtually no nitrogen. In other words the soil is extraordinarily infertile. Also, compounding this problem we can see that the soil is very shallow and, in places, the bare rock is actually showing through. Nowhere here is the soil more than three or four inches (ten centimetres) deep, which means that the plant roots meet the underlying rock very soon. People do find it rather difficult to accept that the richness of the chalk floras is largely due to the infertility of the soil. However, I think that this can be more easily understood by imagining that you are a farmer who has just bought this land. Naturally you want to improve the grazing and to achieve this you dress the grassland with fertilizers, because in that way you will improve the productivity of the sward. It would become more lush and as a result you could graze more sheep on it for a longer period of time. But by improving the growth of the sward, you would at the same time supress the smaller, slow-growing species. There is this inverse relationship between grassland productivity and floristic richness. The result would be that quite rapidly, within one or two years, the number of different species in the grassland would be reduced very dramatically, simply by adding nitrogen and phosphorous fertilizer. So there is the paradox – the richness of the grassland in terms of numbers of species of plants is due primarily to the infertility of the soil.

'But that's only part of the story. Another fascinating aspect, which ecologists are looking at now, is the possibility that the very rich downland insect fauna is also having some influence in maintaining the number of plant species. It works something like this: suppose that you have a plant which has associated with it a number of different insects which feed on nothing else other than that particular species of plant. That plant will have on it a cohort of herbivores that are feeding on its leaves, seeds and so on. Now, when that plant seeds, the seeds will fall at different distances from the plant and it follows that those that fall farthest away will naturally have the greatest chance of escaping the attention of the herbivorous insects simply because they have further to go from the parent plant to find them. This inevitably means that for some species the individual plants are going to be spaced out over the chalk grassland at a distance which represents the resolution of this conflict. If you imagine that all the different species are spaced out in this way, then you will have spaces between the plants of one species that can then be occupied by other species. This helps to increase what is called the "niche" diversity of the grassland. Finally, the sheep grazing, itself, was of great importance. And after the majority of the flocks had disappeared, rabbit grazing partly took over the role up until 1954 when myxomatosis drastically curtailed their numbers. So whilst the infertile soil restricted the size to which any plant could grow from below, the rather unselective grazing of the sheep and rabbits restricted the size to which any individual plant could grow from above, so to speak, by chewing it off. Essentially it is this combination of grazing and soil infertility which is responsible for the very large number of different plants that we can see.

'Now we are left with the sixty-four-thousand-dollar question. Why is it that if you went to an area of grassland on a sandy soil which was similarly grazed and similarly infertile, would you get far fewer species than you do on this chalk soil? I think it is true to say that no-one really knows that answer yet. But it is a fact that, for some reason or other, all over western Europe more species of plant have evolved to grow on chalk soils than have evolved to grow on acid soils, and that is one of the many interesting questions that plant ecologists are researching at the moment.'

We asked David how, if the open landscape and the grassy sward is, in a sense, an artificial creation, did the plants come to be here in the first place?

'That's a lovely question! Where we are sitting now is obviously well below the tree line and only around 400 feet (100 metres) above sea level, so that originally it would have been woodland. As we have noted, this plant community is something that has been brought about by thousands of years of sheep-grazing, and on the South Downs that may be anything up to 5000 years. We know, for example, that by the Neolithic Age man had already cleared a good deal of the woodland cover and had sheep here. However, originally all the plants growing in this turf must have had some sort of natural habitat. It's the old story of where did daisies grow before there were lawns? Here we have a question of the same kind, but on a vast

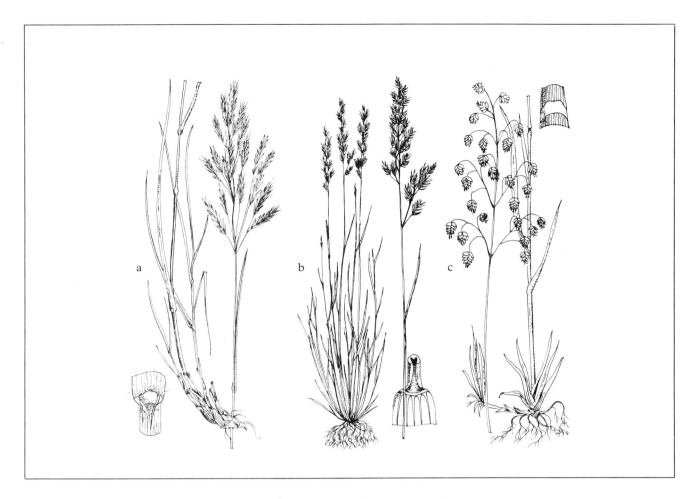

scale. It is possible to resolve the different species that we can see, or many of them, to a more natural type of habitat. A fairly obvious example are chalk cliffs – both inland and sea cliffs. Other species were perhaps plants that you would find in woodland clearings and scrub. Disturbed ground, such as you might find around animal burrows, is another habitat. Plants have always exploited these disturbed or "weedy" areas. Plants have come together from all these diverse habitats to form the very rich matrix that we see here today.

'Now if we look at the species that are growing, there is another interesting point to make which concerns geographical distribution. As we are on a warm south-facing slope and in southern England, it might not be too surprising to find that many of the plants are most at home in southern Europe and here in Britain do not go much further north than the Thames. The round-headed rampion, *Phyteuma tenerum*, is a case in point. It is sometimes called the Pride of Sussex because there is more of it in Sussex than anywhere else, although I think our friends in Dorset might well dispute that. It is a beautiful plant with its head of sky-blue

campanula-like flowers. Fortunately it is quite common in this particular area.

'The flowers that are most often associated in people's minds with the chalk downs are the orchids. Somehow they possess that indefinable fascination of the exotic and are a truly remarkable group of plants. We have more than fifty different species in Britain and, of these, about thirty are found on the chalk hills of southern England. Perhaps the most characteristic is the fragrant orchid, *Gymnadenia conopsea*, with its tall spike of lovely magenta-coloured flowers. Two or three weeks ago this slope was covered with literally hundreds of them, but as you can see they have rather gone over now. Spotted orchids, *Dactylorchis fuchsii*, are also common earlier in the year but they are by no means confined to the chalk. Perhaps the most remarkable looking are those whose flowers mimic the pollinating insect like the bee orchid, *Ophrys apifera*, which can also be found on this hillside given a bit of time and patience. The sepals are a deep rose pink but the lower petal looks just like a bumble-bee, and, indeed, on the Continent, the male bee is fooled by the similarity into mistaking the flower for the female and attempts to mate

Three common grasses of downland: *a* **upright brome,** *Zerna erecta; b* **sheep's fescue,** *Festuca ovina; c* **quaking grass,** *Briza media.*

Above **A male chalk-hill blue,** *Lysandra coridon*, **one of the lovely downland butterflies.**

Left **A bumble bee showing its pollen 'basket'. Some bees have been known to carry 60 per cent of their own weight in pollen.**

Opposite **Any walk across downland on a sunny summer's day will be taken against a background of singing grasshoppers. The 'pegs' on the hind legs which help produce the sound can be clearly seen.**

A mat of the chalkland plantain – *Plantago media* or hoary plantain. This is the only British member of this family that is insect-pollinated and has scented flowers with conspicuous pinkish stamens.

with it, transferring the sticky pollen mass onto its head in the process. When it repeats the experience with another flower cross-pollination is affected. Interestingly enough, bee orchids in Britain are always self-pollinated as the pollinating bee doesn't reach this far north. Other specialities are the tiny, little, yellow musk orchid, *Herminium monorchis*, and the pyramidal orchid, *Anacamptis pyramidalis*, both of which flower rather later in the summer.'

We were thrilled by the idea of being surrounded by such a wealth of plants and decided, for fun, to look at the species immediately around us and see how many we could locate within an area of one square foot. Faced with the challenge David got down on his knees and started counting.

'If we look at the composition of the grassland sward in detail, we can see that it consists of a matrix which is based on three different kinds of grass. Firstly, there's this very fine-leaved grass, sheep's fescue, *Festuca ovina*, which has an almost bristle-like leaf. In the old days of extensive sheep farming it was by far the most abundant of all the grasses on the chalk, which is how it got its name.

'Then, I'm afraid, mixed up with the sheep's fescue on this slope is this much more robust grass, tor grass, *Brachypodium pinnatum*, which has a flat, rather yellow-green leaf that is rough if you pull your fingers down it from the tip to base. It is very invasive and will rapidly take over the sward in the absence of grazing. So it's a thing to watch and not allow to become too abundant as it does swamp a lot of the smaller and less common species.

'The third chalk grass which can become dominant is the upright brome grass, *Zerna*

erecta, which has rather long flat leaves. If it's not in flower you can always recognise it because along the margins of the leaf there is a row of hairs which are very regularly spaced. Each hair is about as long as the leaf base is broad. Mixed up with the grasses is one of the chalk sedges. Sedges are easily told from grasses by the stem which is solid and more or less triangular in cross-section as opposed to being hollow and circular. This one is the carnation sedge, *Carex flacca*, so-called because the leaves are the same colour as those of a carnation. So that makes four species. No doubt if we look more carefully we will turn up some other grasses.

'Yes, there's meadow oat-grass, *Helictotrichon pratense*, which has leaves which are more or less the same colour as the carnation. sedge. However, they are very stiff and narrow and the tip is shaped like the prow of a boat or a monk's cowl. So that's five species of grasses and sedges.

'Here is the prettiest of all the chalk grasses – quaking grass, *Briza media*, which has these very characteristic oval-shaped spikelets that quiver in the wind in a most delightful manner. The leaves of the *Briza* are quite undistinguished; they're not hairy; they're not hooded; they're not ribbed. They are, however, very obviously two-rowed with just a little twist in the leaf which is very characteristic.

'If we look at some of the other plant families, there is a whole wealth of things here. Here's a little white flower with very narrow leaves that are whorled around the stem. It is called squinancywort, *Asperula cynanchica*, and is a relative of the bedstraws. It is a typical plant of these dry chalk slopes. And here we have perhaps the most common and characteristic of all the chalk grassland herbs – salad burnet, *Poterium sanguisorba*. It is a little herbaceous member of the rose family with a compact round head of flowers. It used to be put in salads and drink and is still sometimes cultivated as a herb. And here we have the only really true chalk grassland member of the umbellifers or cow parsley family, the burnet saxifrage, *Pimpinella saxifraga*. It has a little white umbel of flowers that look very attractive. There are two or three members of the daisy or composite family here as well. This family has many species that puzzle people no end as they all look like dandelions at a first glance and are apparently impossible to differentiate. This one is a common member – the rough hawkbit, *Leontodon hispidus*. It has a very hairy leaf and if you look at the hairs under a lens you will find that they are T- or Y-shaped. There is the yellow flower-head with the very hairy involucre-bracts beneath. Amongst these is another species of yellow composite, the mouse-ear hawkweed, *Hieracium pilosella*, which has very distinctive leaves with this pure white felt underneath, no teeth around the margin and these extraordinary long hairs on the upper surface. The mouse-ear hawkweed has much paler flowers than the hawkbit. I think we have actually got a third species here which I hadn't noticed – the hairy hawkbit, *Leontodon taraxacoides*. This is much less hairy on the upper part of the stem and is smaller than the rough hawkbit.

'The little purple flowers here belong to wild thyme, *Thymus drucei*, which occurs throughout Britain on well-drained soils. Incidentally, there is another species which flowers later in the year on these southern chalklands – large thyme, *T. pulegioides*. It is slightly bigger and has a more noticeable scent.

'Now we have to look around a little bit more. Ah, here is a member of a very important family on the chalk slopes – the legume or pea family. This is horseshoe vetch, *Hippocrepis comosa*. It has leaves composed of four or five pairs of leaflets and, unlike a true vetch, a terminal leaflet instead of a tendril. It has a yellow flower which is similar to birds-foot trefoil, *Lotus corniculatus*. But the significance of horseshoe vetch is that it is the food plant of the larvae of one of the most beautiful of all the chalk downland butterflies – the adonis blue. Other members of this plant group are important to other butterflies and we will look at that later on. The birds-foot trefoil has five leaflets and is so named because the fruits supposedly spread out like the foot of a fowl – if you have enough imagination.

'There's the round-headed rampion and here is a seedling of the small scabious, *Scabiosa columbaria*, with its toothed basal leaves. Now this is a nice plant to have in flower in our square – yellow rattle, *Rhinanthus minor*. It has this yellow flower and large calyx that becomes inflated later in the year when you can hear the seeds rattling inside it. Here is the leaf of another member of the rose family, the dropwort, *Filipendula vulgaris*, which is the chalkland equivalent of the meadowsweet, *F. ulmaria*, of damp meadows and riversides. That makes nineteen species so far.

Above **A pair of chalk-hill blue butterflies mating. The resulting eggs will be laid singly on the stems of horse-shoe vetch,** *Hippocrepis comosa.*

Left **The tiny flowers of squinancywort,** *Asperula cynanchica.* **This typical downland member of the bedstraws is often found growing on ant hills.**

'We are almost sitting – but I'm glad to say not quite – on two very vicious-looking rosettes of the stemless thistle, *Cirsium acualon*. It is one of those plants which is essentially southern European and its distribution in Britain is very characteristic, stopping almost dead at a line drawn from the Humber to the Severn. If you were to carry out a survey of the numbers of plants on this south-facing slope and compare that with a similar survey on the north-facing slope across the valley you would find that there are more plants on this side. So this thistle is really rather precise in its climatic preferences.

'This is the rosette of a typical chalkland member of the plantain family, hoary plantain, *Plantago media*. Unlike other plantains which are wind pollinated this plant is insect pollinated and has scented flowers with these lovely pale-pink stamens. Right next door is the rosette of the much more common narrow-leaved or ribwort plantain, *P. lanceolata*. Finally, here is the little white flower of the fairy or purging flax, *Linum catharticum*. It is a tiny plant with glossy, hairless, egg-shaped leaves in opposite pairs up the stem and these minute white flowers. That gives us a total of twenty-two species, not bad at all.'

We agreed with David that identifying that many species of plant in one square foot of a random piece of turf was a convincing result. However, having hinted at the butterflies in the area we were eager for him to tell us more.

'The adonis blue butterfly, *Lysandra bellargus*, is still, I'm happy to say, fairly abundant in this particular locality. Sadly, however, this species, which is restricted chiefly to southern England, is rapidly disappearing from most areas as more and more of the old chalkland turf becomes "improved" or ploughed up. The adonis blue has two broods in the year. The first emerges at the end of May or the beginning of June and is in flight all through June. The second appears at the end of July or the beginning of August. So, unfortunately, we are in the gap between the two broods! The males are coloured a very intense blue, much more so than the common blue, *Polyommatus icarus*. They also have a much more distinctive white border to the wings which is transversed by fine black bands where the veins cross the wing. The females are very drab in comparison being predominantly brown in colour. They lay their eggs singly on the undersurface of one of the terminal leaflets of the horse-shoe vetch. They choose plants some distance apart as the caterpillars are cannibalistic. The short stubby caterpillars which are now developing will pupate and the butterflies emerge at the end of the month in August. Another rather special blue butterfly that we find here is the chalkhill blue, *Lysandra coridon*, which is not quite so uncommon as the adonis blue. Its range extends a little further north in Britain. The caterpillars feed on both the horse-shoe vetch and on another member of the legume family – the birds-foot trefoil. However, it does not compete with the adonis as they feed and emerge at different times, having only one brood which flies during July so if we are lucky we might see some. The males are much paler than the adonis males; they are a kind of powder blue with a distinct dark border to the wing.

'A third species of blue butterfly is the common blue, which is much more generally distributed, and, having two or three broods each year, can be seen in most months from May to September. The caterpillars of this species feed on birds-foot trefoil. Also in this general area are two other members of the "blues" – the small blue, *Cupido minimus*, and the brown argus, *Aricia agestis*. The small blue is a tiny beast, with a wingspan of only 20 millimetres as opposed to the common blue which can reach over 35 millimetres. It is darker in colour than the other three and feeds on another member of the pea family, the kidney vetch, *Anthyllis vulneraria*. Finally we come to one more blue which is brown, the brown argus! Its caterpillars feed on rock rose, *Helianthemum chamaecistus*, a typical chalk grassland flower, and has two broods, one in May and another in July.

Right At the bottom of the hill we found several flowering spikes of yellow-wort, *Blackstonia perfoliata*. This plant is easily recognisable with its bright yellow gentian-like flowers and fused opposite pairs of leaves. The whole plant has a distinctive greyish colour.

Below A large ant-hill garlanded with thyme, *Thymus*. The larger and more numerous the ant-hills, the older the grassland is likely to be.

A pair of six-spot burnet moths, *Zygaena filipendulae*, pairing outside a cocoon high up on a grass stem. These brightly coloured moths are day-flying and can often be seen amongst the longer grass on downland slopes.

'The more you look at these insects, the more you start to ask the obvious questions and then one begins to realise how little we know about them. For instance, why is it that in this family, the adonis blue has a blue male and a brown female; the common blue has a blue male and a bluish-brown female; the brown argus, a brown male and a brown female; while the large blue has a blue male and a blue female? No-one knows the answer.

'There is one aspect of the natural history of these insects that we do know something about and that is the relationship between the blues and ants. This is most extreme in the large blue, *Maculinea arion*, which recently became extinct in Britain. Nevertheless, the chalkhill blue also has a fascinating link with the ants, which actually search out the caterpillars and may carry them to a location close to their nest placing them on a suitable plant of birds-foot trefoil. In return for the protection the ants afford the larvae, they "milk" a gland on its back which produces a sweet juice that the ants will seem to do anything for. Indeed, in the large blue they take the caterpillar into their nest where it feeds on the ants' own larvae. It is all quite astonishing.

'A lot of people are probably most aware of the butterflies when they are out walking. But these chalk slopes have many other interesting insects. Perhaps one of the most obvious groups are the grasshoppers. The noise of their "singing" is all around us. This order of insects as a whole is tropical and even though we have a rather poor grasshopper fauna in Britain, you may be surprised to learn that we have eleven species. The ones that we can hear singing are all males as the females are silent. This "singing" should properly be called stridulating as it is not produced through the mouth like a bird's song but by rubbing a series of pegs on the inside of their hind legs against the hard outside edge of the wing cases. But then, like birds, each species has its own distinctive song, so if you know your grasshoppers' repertoire, you can impress your friends by naming them after hearing the song. If you listen carefully you can hear three different species right now. The one that sounds like a high-pitched angry bee with a continuous "zzzzzzz" noise is the stripe-winged grasshopper, *Stenobothrus lineatus*. It has a distribution which is similar to the round-headed rampion in that it is distinctly southern and does not occur much further north than the

Thames, except for a few isolated localities. Here, it is very abundant on the nice warm south-facing slope – but is generally an uncommon species. Then there are two much more widely distributed grasshoppers. First, there is the common green grasshopper, *Omacestus viridulus*, which sounds for all the world like a free-wheeling bicycle, and the meadow grasshopper, *Chorthippus parallelus*, which makes a rather feeble noise, "praah", "praah".

'Snails are another group of invertebrates that are abundant in chalk grassland. These molluscs need calcium carbonate with which to construct their shells, and what habitat has more of it than chalk? If you dig around at the base of the grasses it is quite easy to come up with a handful of snails. I have two species right here. One of them is very common and found on all types of calcium-rich habitats – chalk and limestone grassland, as well as calcium-rich sand dunes. It is called *Candidula intersecta*, and is a small, flat, banded shell. In contrast, this other one has a very different shape, like a miniature-spire and is much less common. It is called *Cochlicella acuta*, and is, like so many of the plants and animals here, more or less restricted to the southern chalkland. This one does creep up around the west coast and can be found in sand dunes. There are often similarities between sand dune habitats and chalk grassland simply because dunes collect a lot of calcium carbonate from washed up marine shells.

'A third species that we should find here is called the round-mouthed snail, *Pomatias elegans*. It looks just like a little land periwinkle and is one of the two British land snails that has an operculum – a little 'trap-door' on the underside of the foot of the snail which seals it in when it retracts into the shell. Most of our land snails secrete a membrane across the shell if they really want to shut themselves off.'

We decided it was time to move on and have a look at the animals and plants lower down the slope. So, making sure not to put our hands on the spines of the stemless thistles, we clambered up and set off down the hill. A common blue butterfly fluttered quickly past us but there was no sign of any lingering adonis blues. However, we were to be luckier later in the year on another stretch of downland further west. The grass lower down the slope was taller but before we went any further we stopped by some odd mounds which turned out to be large anthills. Were these to be expected here? David was quite emphatic.

'Yes, anthills are very characteristic of old chalk grassland slopes and even have their own specialised plant and animal communities. The ant responsible for these is usually the yellow meadow ant, *Lasius flavus*. And although it looks fairly quiet at the moment if you disturbed it or even sat on it you would soon find out that it was very active! Interestingly, the plants growing on the top of the anthill often differ from the surrounding grassland. It has a much shorter sward than round about. This is partly because the rabbits tend to chew them down. They also use them regularly as latrines as can be seen by the large number of droppings here. There is a higher density of sheep's fescue than elsewhere and here is a common grass that we have not seen so far – crested hairgrass, *Koeleria cristata*. It is one of those grasses that extends right into eastern Europe and is an important grass of the steppes. Typical of these anthills, there is also a nice mixture of wild thyme and squinancywort.

'Anthills are one of the few examples that you can find in nature of a regular pattern of distribution. If you were, for instance, to measure the distance between these anthills, you would find that they were spread in a fairly uniform fashion about the hill. Another interesting feature of anthills is the communities of other animals that they support. If we were to be able to look inside one of them we might find a very exciting little woodlice called *Platyarthrus hoffmannseggi*, which is both blind and colourless. There is also a subterranean snail called *Ceciliodes acicula*, which is only about three millimetres long and also colourless. One of the few places that you are likely to find it is in an ant's nest. A fascinating book was written on the subject in the 1920s by H. Donisthorpe entitled *The Guests of British Ants*, and was just as large as the monograph which preceded it on the biology of the British ants themselves.'

We now moved on further down into the ranker grass. As we cut through it we noticed several new species of butterflies flying up in front of us. David took up the story.

'These are quite different from the ones that we saw further up the slope. The reason for this is primarily to do with the longer grass on which their larvae feed. The most obvious one today and to my mind perhaps the most beautiful of all our British butter-

flies, is the marbled white, *Melanargia galathea*. Although it is only black and white, the lovely marbling of the two colours, particularly when it is sitting with its wings closed and the sun is shining through it from behind, is really a most atmospheric and beautiful sight. Surprisingly the marbled white is not a member of the Pieridae or white family, which includes the cabbage white, but belongs to the Satyridae or brown family. So it is more closely related to the much more drab meadow brown and gatekeepers. A characteristic of this family is the eye-like mark towards the apex of the forewing and if you look carefully you can see that it does have such a mark. The caterpillars feed on grasses so why they should be confined to calcareous soils is a bit of a puzzle. But like some of our blues they are a southern species and are generally found south of a line drawn from the Wash to the Severn.

'The marbled white has evolved a very interesting egg-laying technique. Whilst egg-laying, female insects are particularly at risk from predators as they have to be motionless for a fair amount of time while they are laying

A mating pair of marbled white butterflies, *Melanargia galathea*, amongst the ranker grass and knapweeds at the hill bottom. These beautiful insects are confined to the downlands of southern England.

Above **A very different type of habitat with some very different flowers. This is the edge of a nearby cornfield, which has been colonised by a whole array of arable 'weed' species including poppies,** *Papaver,* **and scentless mayweed,** *Tripleurospermum inodorum.*

Opposite **If one looks closely enough there is a lot to discover in almost any stretch of countryside. This striking photograph of the flower head of a mayweed shows not only the flower's extraordinary structure but also a hover-fly and below it a diminutive thrip.**

their eggs. Most butterflies have to to search for their food plant and then carefully place the eggs on the leaf. The marbled white, however, does not have to search out a particular plant as the caterpillar feeds on most grasses and therefore the female can simply drop her eggs at random over the grassy sward without settling at all. The chances of an egg not falling on a piece of grass in a place like this are negligible. The only other British butterfly that uses this technique is the ringlet, *Aphantopus hyperanthus,* which also feeds on grasses.

'Flying around us is what must be the commonest British butterfly – the meadow brown, *Maniola jurtina.* You can find it on almost any stretch of rough grassland or hedgebank. Although they are so abundant, you will not find the caterpillars that easily. This is because the caterpillars of all the browns are fairly well camouflaged and during the day they drop to the base of the grasses, only climbing up to feed at night.

'A third species of brown butterfly is flitting about just here. This is the smallest of

the tribe – the small heath, *Coenonympha pamphilus.* This must be one of the most widely distributed of all our butterflies, being found almost the length and breadth of the British Isles on downs and heaths, waste-ground and even mountain sides. It is a lovely tawny brown colour with the typical 'eyes' on the forewing. Its larvae are also grass-feeders.

'As well as the butterflies we have been turning up a few day-flying moths. Not all moths fly exclusively at night, and perhaps the most obvious of these are the burnet moths. There are two common species, the six-spot burnet, *Zygaena filipendulae,* the commonest of the two, and the five spot burnet, *Z. trifolii.* The larvae of these moths feed on members of the pea family, particularly birds-foot trefoil. The adult moths have this very distinct scarlet and dark bronze-green warning coloration. They are extremely poisonous and have a very unpleasant taste so predators soon learn to avoid them. The adults are a common sight over downland such as this in mid-summer and are especially attracted to the flower of wild marjoram, *Origanum vulgare,* and basil, *Clinopodium vulgare.*'

Further along the slope our attention was caught by a fairly tall flower with striking yellow flowers. We asked David to identify the plant.

'This is yellow-wort, *Blackstonia perfoliata;* it is actually a yellow flowered member of the gentian family. These primrose yellow flowers open during mid-day and are arranged in a loose head. The most characteristic feature of this plant, however, is the leaves. These are arranged in pairs up the stem and are joined at the base so that the stalk appears to grow up through them. Hence the Latin name, *perfoliata.* Again, it is a plant, like so many we have seen today, that is confined to calcareous soils in southern Britain.'

We started to make our way back to the cars along the valley bottom but first of all we strolled along an area of scrub. As we approached it we could hear a most peculiar song. We scanned the area with our binoculars and soon located a dumpy-looking brown bird. David pointed it out.

'Just there, sitting on one of the fence posts. It is a corn bunting with its extraordinary song, which I call "scritcheting" – and I don't mean that to sound complimentary! The corn bunting is by no means classed amongst the world's best songsters.

Nevertheless, to me, its song does sum up the feeling and the mood of the summer chalk country of the South Downs. The corn bunting is polygamous; he has quite a large territory within which several females will nest. Although he places himself rather prominently within sight of the nests it is no good watching him in order to discover the nest sites, as he never flies to the nest to feed the females while they are incubating. Corn buntings have a characteristic heavy flight and let their rather pale-coloured legs trail behind them.'

'We were now amongst the area of scrub near the top of the valley. It presented an almost impenetrable barrier of gorse, *Ulex europeaus*, hawthorn, *Crategus monogyna* and bramble, *Rubrus fruticosus,* but was obviously ideal for nesting birds so we sat down for a while to see what we could.

'We are in the middle of a hot afternoon when most bird song has ceased but we can still hear a fair amount of calling. Probably this type of scrub has one of the highest densities of breeding birds of any habitat we have. We've heard linnets, yellowhammers, dunnocks, wrens and the inevitable blackbirds. The only common warbler is the whitethroat. It suffered a decline in its numbers a few years ago but this was nothing to do with the breeding success here in Britain but resulted from a severe drought in the Sahel region of the Sahara where our whitethroats spend the winter. The numbers appear to be picking up again now, which is certainly good news. We can hear its rather throaty, chuckling song just behind us.'

We walked on up to the ridge of the hill where suddenly the scene completely changed. In front of us was a vast expanse of wheat rippling in the gentle breeze; a vivid contrast to the scrub and old grassland behind us. The only noise was the gentle hiss of ripening heads of wheat brushing against each other; quite unlike the busy hum of activity we had just left behind. But every cloud has a silver lining, as they say, and this great area certainly had a very colourful one, as David explained.

'We have a great sea of wheat in front of us – one of the main reasons why so much of the old chalk downland sward has disappeared. Beside us is an even bigger sea of barley. Of course, the Downs are very productive when it comes to growing cereals and the farmers are always concerned to increase their cereal production. However, if you look around the edges of these vast fields you can

still find the remnants of the old rich arable flora – in other words, the weeds. These have managed to escape the effects of the herbicides with which the crops are dressed. Some of the weeds are now becoming a little resistant to the herbicides.

'There is really a quite rich and interesting flora just here. In particular, the poppies are worth looking for. To some people they conjure up a picture of the past. There are actually five species of red poppy in Britain but the one which most of us come across is the common poppy, *Papaver rhoeas*. This eye-catching plant is the one with the big crinkly red petals with a smooth round fruit capsule. Here we have one of the four rarer species as well – the prickly poppy, *P. argemone.* The flowers, which are similar but smaller than the common poppy, are over now but we can see the main distinguishing feature – the long bristly fruit capsule. I was up here a few weeks ago and there were actually two other species of poppy here as

well – so it is worth looking for them.

'There are many other weed species here. For instance, here is a large patch of the introduced pineapple or rayless mayweed, *Matricaria matricaroides*. It looks rather like a big daisy with all the white ray florets pulled off. Like so many arable weeds it is an accidental introduction and originates from South America. And here is a mix of plants which one might expect to find: knotgrass, *Polygonum aviculare*; red bartsia, *Odontites verna*; common field speedwell, *Veronica persica* (although an abundant weed it is, in fact, a native of Asia Minor that was introduced accidentally over two centuries ago) and wall speedwell, *V. arvensis*. Weeds are highly specialised plants that are well adapted to their mode of life. They have to be able to take advantage of bare, disturbed ground that appears in unpredictable places at unpredictable times. In order to do this successfully they have evolved a reproductive strategy that is different from most species. They invest in vast numbers of seeds which spread very widely so that at least some fall where there is a bare patch of fertile soil. Because of this high investment in seeds they are short-lived annuals. A short life, but a happy one! The other point about weeds is that quite often they are self-fertilising, so that if only one isolated plant becomes established it can still produce fertile seed and a new generation of plants. They also have a long flowering season with some in flower almost the whole year round.'

We turned away from the edge of the apparently endless wheat field and took one last look over at the downland valley in which we had spent such an invigorating afternoon. But reluctantly it was time for us to depart and as we drove back alongside the great cereal fields, the dramatic contrast brought home how important it is to preserve the few remaining areas of old chalk downland with their very special communities of animals and plants.

A contented herd of cattle quietly browsing in the afternoon sun. At the top of the ridge the encroaching scrub is very much in evidence. Without the constant attention of animals like these cattle the slope would soon be taken over by coarser plants.

A downland walk in late summer

Take a trip to your local library or museum and ask to see a geological map of the British Isles. Check up which, of all the many colours, represents chalk and see the way in which this special rock is distributed across the face of Britain. It sweeps in a great series of arcs, interrupted in places, across and around south east England. Wherever this soft rock forms the basis of the landscape there is the promise of downland walks with all their flowers and insects. Of course, much of the chalk is now covered with vast fields of cereals or even urban sprawl but, even here, the influence of the chalk is there as a skeletal whiteness in newly ploughed ground, a gentleness of contour or indicated simply by the twisted liana-like stems of old man's beard festooning hedges and fences in forgotten corners. The Downs of Hampshire and Dorset, though not as famous as those further to the east, are of great beauty and interest, especially where the chalk abuts onto the acid sandstone heaths producing some of the sharpest contrasts both in land-use and in natural history. All this spiced with that special western coastal climate means that a grassland walk holds much in store.

In spring the downland slopes seem to be dotted with yellow flowers and, as the seasons progress, the colours turn more to blue until, in the late summer, the predominance of scabious and knapweeds turn the slopes a rich purple.

A downland walk in late summer
with
Paul Toynton

The landscape in almost any area of Britain, whether it is open grassland or woodland, a winding river valley or dry heath, is the product not simply of the geology and natural vegetation but also the combined influences of thousands of years of habitation by man. If you walk down any street in a town or city you will find modern houses next to older buildings; you may find a whole row of Elizabethan houses around one corner and then a Norman church, tucked away in a quiet side road. If you can read the signs, the open countryside is just like this – a pre-historic burial mound on a hill, ancient Saxon ridge and furrow contours showing up beneath modern cereal crops, medieval watermeadows with their dykes and channels being grazed by cattle next to a wood planted up with conifers by an ambitious Victorian landowner. In order to appreciate the land-scape today and importantly, in a nature reserve, to manage it successfully, this historical perspective on the countryside is important. It often points to the reason for the local distribution of certain plants and, unfortunately, more often explains their disappearance. To see how man has in-fluenced a particular piece of grassland over the ages and to find out how to tackle the very real problems of maintaining some of the richness of our grassland animals and plants, we visited a reserve at the east end of the Dorset Downs in late summer. Our guide and expert for the day was the reserve

warden, Paul Toynton, who has had many years of experience in managing chalk down-land.

We started our walk at the bottom of the down where the grass was fairly tall. Before we set out across the reserve towards the higher areas we asked Paul to tell us a little of the background to his work on the down.

'This area of downland is really an island amidst a sea of arable farmland. If you look over the borders of the reserve in almost every direction you will find fields of wheat and barley. The reason that this area has survived the recent agricultural expansion is that it is registered common land, which means that no one person has the right to enclose and plough it up. An extensive tract of downland, like this, is very important to preserve as the number of areas that have escaped the modern plough or have been re-seeded, is still decreasing.

'Not long ago it was often thought that by simply designating a site such as this a nature reserve, it would be sufficient to preserve it. Some early chalkland reserves were managed along the lines of creating sanctuaries where active management of the sites was not given the attention that it has here. This was partly a result of the obvious reluctance of conser-vationists to see the flowers that they were supposed to be preserving, being trampled or eaten. It was also partly born out of the notion that the classic short grassland sward was automatically kept in check and al-

Opposite left **The dense flower head of a typical downland umbel – wild carrot,** *Daucus carota.* **Notice the single pink flower in the centre of the head.**

Centre **The farming of these Welsh mountain sheep is a vital part of the management of downland reserves as only by careful grazing can the short turf required by so many of the plants and insects be maintained.**

Left **The seed heads of agrimony,** *Agrimonia eupatoria,* **with their hooked spines.**

though it was grazed by rabbits and before that by sheep, there was no need to do anything. Indeed, after the crash of the rabbit population in the early 1950s, following the introduction of myxomatosis, the flowers bloomed in profusion for a short while. However, today, all too often, we can see the results of lack of management on open grassland areas that are no longer fully utilised for agriculture – scrub has invaded very rapidly and whole sites have lost their profusion of flowers and insects and become, in effect, woodland.

'When I first came here just over five years ago large areas of the site, particularly where the soils were deeper, were dominated by upright brome grass, *Zerna erecta,* and dense scrub had encroached over significant sections. My dog had to stand on her hind legs to see the sheep! I honestly thought that large parts were so far gone that they would take many years to recover. But since then by the selective reintroduction of sheep grazing we have made quite a difference, as you shall see.'

We struck out across into the knee high grassland which, although it was late August, was still laced with flowers. As we made our way along, Paul pointed out some of the key species.

'This first area is not typical of chalk downland as we have quite deep, fertile soils and consequently a greater show of grasses and few of the really specialist chalk down-land species. As we head towards the hill you will notice how the grass becomes shorter and the variety of flowers increases. Some of the tall plants grow well here because the area is grazed in winter and not during the growing season. For instance, we have some typical grassland umbels along this stretch. The tall plant with the yellow flowers is wild parsnip, *Pastinaca sativa.* There is also wild carrot, *Daucus carota,* which starts off with this dense flat flowerhead with usually a single pink floret right in the middle. When it is in fruit it curls up at the edge to form this lovely bird's nest-shaped head. The wild carrot can always be told apart from the other umbels as it has these three-pointed bracts underneath the flowerhead. A plant which is adding a purple colour to some areas is the greater knapweed, *Centaurea scabiosa.* This is a great favourite with the butterflies and this summer we have been treated to the sight of seven or eight marbled whites, *Melanargia galathea,* and two or three dark green fritil-laries, *Argynnis aglaja,* all on the one plant! At this time of year there are still a lot of meadow browns, *Maniola jartina,* in this longer grass. Apart from the upright brome there is a great deal of cocksfoot, *Dactylis glomerata,* here, which again is not typical of the true chalk downs. Now this is our third grassland umbel – burnet-saxifrage, *Pimpinella saxifraga,* which is comparatively late flowering and has these very fine divided leaves. Unlike the carrot it has no bracts. The

A view across one of the flatter areas of the reserve. The shiny patch of grass in the centre is a spreading mat of tor grass, *Brachypodium pinnatum*.

basal leaves are broader, looking rather like those of dropwort, *Filipendula vulgaris*, which we should see later.

'When we first came here, one plant that was still surviving amidst this long grass was the agrimony, *Agrimonia eupatoria*, which, although it has finished flowering this year, has these seed heads with hooked spines. So, after walking through this for a while, you will find there are quite a few hanging onto your clothes.

'We've now moved up to an area where the grass is slightly shorter and one of the most noticeable features is the spreading patches of tor grass, *Brachypodium pinnatum*. This grass is a very serious problem, as it is very sharp and unpalatable so it must be kept in check. Trampling helps to control it therefore we try to arrange it so that the sheep graze it in early spring when it is still tender and they then trample it down and graze it. It seems to do especially well after burning, so we have to be careful to avoid this.

'Two plants are making quite a show here: the mauve flowers of small scabious, *Scabiosa*

Above **A classic autumn flower of chalk grassland – the autumn gentian,** *Gentianella amarella* – **next to the small white and yellow flowers of eyebright,** *Euphrasia.*

Left **Another umbel of chalk grassland is this burnet-saxifrage** *Pimpinella saxifraga,* **which is clearly showing its strap-like upper leaves and bractless umbels of white flowers.**

columbaria, and the darker reddish-purple flowers of hardhead or black knapweed, *Centaurea nigra.* The black knapweed can often be told from its cousin, the greater knapweed, by the lack of enlarged outer florets but interestingly, here most of the population does have these, so one has to look at the leaves, which are simple in the black knapweed and deeply lobed in the greater, to tell them apart.

'Although these ranker areas are often dismissed by botanists as they are not as rich as the short turf sites for plants, they do provide an imortant habitat for many grass-land insects. If one looks at the structure of this grass, which has a lot of living space both vertically and horizontally, you can see that it offers a humid environment for such things as small plant-sucking bugs, weevils, milli-pedes and woodlice, that would otherwise suffer from problems of dessication in short grass.'

We had now arrived by an area that was cordoned off by low electrified wire netting. Inside, were the real workers on the down, Paul's flock of sheep – 120 Welsh mountain sheep. We asked Paul to tell us about their use.

'These sheep are quite small, but they are hardy and easier to manage than the lowland breeds of sheeps, which can be twice as large. They are very tough and do not need supplementary feed during the winter, which is ideal for us. This type of sheep is frequently used on reserves now, but it has to be remembered that we use them in a very different way to a farmer, at least, initially. A farmer has very different aims; he puts sheep on a down because he wants them to fatten up as soon as possible. So he will move them around as soon as the grass is beginning to become short. He will also graze them all summer, across as wide an area as possible, which means on a down such as this, as soon as the orchids came up they would be eaten off. Now, from a conservation point of view, what we want the sheep to do is to keep the turf short and, where it has become over-grown, that means that we will keep the sheep fairly hungry so that they will eat the rough grasses down. Also, we have to study the plant distribution in the reserve very carefully so that the sheep are grazing the appropriate areas at the various seasons, which often means taking them off some of the better areas during peak summer

months. Unfortunately you have to sacrifice some flowers as the maximum period for growth in the grasses is in the early summer and if that is not grazed back, the low-growing plants would be shaded out. We use these electrified enclosures to control the sheep. This means that we can divide the reserve up into compartments that need various degrees of grazing, depending on their current state, and graze some areas very hard whilst others we might only graze very slightly. The effects of this are carefully monitored so that we can achieve the most out of our sheep. At the moment we are still grazing these areas quite hard during the summer and are already, just within four seasons, starting to see a tremendous increase in the diversity of plants and their attendant insects. The grass here is mostly under 15 centimetres (6 inches) high and the upright brome, which was almost totally dominant back at the start of our walk, is now much less so. We even have the familiar anthills starting to show through.'

We now moved up to look at the steep side of the down where there was only a thin covering of soil. Here we began to find some of the species that we had seen earlier on the South Downs – sheep's fescue, *Festuca ovina*, mouse-eared hawkweed, *Pilosella*

A common feature of many areas of downland is the presence of prehistoric earthworks such as these two bell-barrows, which mark the site of a Bronze Age burial ground.

officinarum, salad burnet, *Poterium sangui-sorba*, stemless thistle, *Cirsium acaulon*, squinancywort, *Asperula cynanchica* and glaucous sedge or carnation grass, *Carex flacca*. Paul pointed out that if one looked carefully enough we would probably find over thirty species in a square metre. There were, however, some plants on this short turf that were new to us. Paul told us something about them.

'A plant that is just coming out now is the autumn gentian or fellwort, *Gentianella amarella*, which will flower for another two or three weeks. If one looks closely at it, one can see that it has these typical gentian-like pinkish-purple flowers. They always look as if they are about to open further, but I'm afraid that is as far as they go. They occur here in large numbers but it never really covers the ground in the flood of colour that you might expect. A significant amount of the ground cover is made up of a sedge, *Carex humilis*, dwarf sedge. Although this sedge is abundant here, it has a strangely limited western distribution in Britain, even though it has a central distribution on the continent. It has been suggested that the reason for its distribution being restricted to Dorset, Wiltshire and Somerset with a few outlying populations, is that its original habitat before the clearance of the lowland forest was limestone cliffs, such as in Somerset and the Avon Gorge, and that it only managed to spread so far before the open chalk or limestone community it needed became dominated by other species. The plant is very wispy with the thin leaves curling back on themselves.

'There are two autumn flowering orchids that we might see – the tiny frog orchid *Coeloglossum viride* and autumn ladies' tresses, *Spiranthes spiralis*. Both are very different from the showy orchids of mid-summer, so they will need a bit of searching out.

'However, before we do that, as we are now near the top of the down, we could stop and have a general look at the view and, perhaps, discuss the history of this stretch of land.

'We are well below the natural treeline here, so it is safe to assume that all this area was woodland before the coming of man. When man arrived he found that the chalk hills were drier and easier to work than the heavy and damper soils of the valleys, so the first land to be cleared and colonised were these downs. There must have been a tremendous number of people living in these dry uplands as there are numerous prehistoric settlements, ditches and burial mounds scattered in the region, the most famous of which are probably the stone circles and earthworks at Avebury and Stonehenge in Wiltshire. The majority of the woodland would have been cleared as much as three thousand years ago, probably by a combination of burning, cutting and grazing. Large areas would have undoubtedly been ploughed. Later on, in Iron Age times, the development of heavier implements enabled man to move down to the heavier soils and clear the forests there. Probably, the chalk grasslands became more important, then, as grazing land rather than arable. However, there has always been a degree of interchangeability between corn and sheep, depending on the economics of the time. In this area, during medieval times, the area we walked up through was ploughed and when the sun is low enough you can still see the strips of the broad ridge and furrow plough lines. Some areas, which would not have been accessible to the traditional methods of ploughing, would have always remained as grazing land. And it is in relation to this history of thousands of years of grazing that the rich grassland sward that we can see today, has developed.

A tiny frog orchid, *Coeloglossum viride*, standing no higher than some of the surrounding grasses. This is one of the orchids that you really have to search on your hands and knees to find!

Above **The carline thistle,** *Carlina vulgaris,* **with its distinctive 'everlasting' flowers. These straw-coloured flower heads will last well into the autumn.**

'The downs here have traces of the management of man as far back as the Bronze Age. For instance, this low hummock we are standing next to, is a Bronze Age barrow. These are a very common feature of downland and indicate the presence of a sacred area, uually where the dead have been laid. They take a wide variety of forms, some have the simple upturned "bowl" form that we can see here. Others were more complex, such as the bell-barrows, which also have a ditch and sometimes an outer bank. They vary considerably in size from this comparatively small one to over thirty metres in diameter. They were often constructed in groups, for example, there is an area to the west of here where there are almost thirty together.

'From a later period we have a very impressive linear earthwork, originating in the Romano-British period. It runs for about three and a half miles (5·6 kilometres) and the theory is that it connects two areas of very dense scrub which were inpenetrable to horse-drawn troops. It runs along the site of a Bronze Age boundary bank and around 300 AD it was built up to be used first against raiders and then against the Saxon advance into Dorset. Botanically it is very interesting as we shall see later on. As we have discussed, we have signs of medieval ploughing in the flatter areas. Then further out, half of the downland was ploughed during the last war as an emergency measure and continued to be ploughed until about 1956. So the grassland in that area is no more than 26 years old, as opposed to the grassland on the dyke, which is perhaps 1600 years old. There is a close link between the richness of the vegetation and the age of the turf, which means that

Centre **The species-rich short turf of the ancient dyke. These old earthworks are often excellent places to discover interesting plants as the grassy sward may well have been left undisturbed, except for grazing, for as long as the date of the original construction itself.**

the reserve has a tremendous variety of chalk grassland and also gives an ideal opportunity to study the recolonisation of the recently ploughed sections.

'As if that isn't enough, we have some superb examples of chalk heath on some of the more acid soils, so don't be too surprised if you find clumps of heather and gorse growing along the top here. However, a more typical feature of these areas is the chalkland scrub. We have tried to contain it by selective cutting, as well as browsing by the sheep. It is particularly good for bird life so it is important to keep some of it. Up on the top here we have some inpenetrable stands of gorse, *Ulex europaeus*, on the chalk heath areas, but the main component of the scrub on the reserve is a mix of hawthorn, *Crataegus monogyna*, blackthorn or sloe, *Prunus spinosa*, privet, *Ligustrum vulgare*, buckthorn, *Rhamnus catharticus*, wayfaring tree, *Viburnum lan-*

Above **Dogwood,** *Cornus sanguinea,* **in full autumn colour with its red stem and leaves and glossy black fruits. This shrub is common on chalk downland and can be very invasive so it has to be constantly kept in check by cutting and grazing.**

tana and spindle, *Euonymus europaeus*, with blackberries, *Rubus fruticosus*, forming a secondary layer. Before the Second World War, there would have been very little scrub apart from the odd hawthorn bush and, although the sheep farming had declined, it wasn't until the mid-fifties, with the disappearance of the rabbits, that the scrub really moved in. Now we are trying to make the best of it without losing too much open habitat.

'Here we have a wayfaring tree, that has these odd oval fruits which are bright red at first then quickly turn black and shrivel. Next to it is wild privet, which many people fail to recognise although it is a relative of the garden privet. This wild species has longer narrower leaves. There is quite an impressive list of birds that nest in these scrubby thickets, particularly warblers, which seem to like the dense cover they provide. We cut the shrub in rotation so that it doesn't become too tall and open. Nightingales, especially, seem to like the areas where there is a thick understorey of blackthorn and hawthorn.'

We now made our way along past two impressive round barrows towards the southern end of the dyke. We could see the line of the earthwork stretching away across the grassland. As we stood there we tried to imagine what it must have been like all those hundreds of years ago with the invading Saxons and the Celtic princes trying to hold them back. The scene looked so peaceful yet that dyke may have been the site of many bloody conflicts. Today, however, it is the haunt of birds and butterflies, is garlanded with traveller's-joy and carpeted with flowers. I wonder what the Celts would have thought about our present fear of invading scrub!

As we walked down on to the east facing bank, Paul began to pick out some of the flowers that were growing. One plant he was keen to show us was the frog orchid. Even though he knew approximately where they were, it still needed a search almost on our knees before we found these extraordinary little plants.

'Here is a colony of frog orchids. The flowers of these plants are a browny-red colour but some are much greener. The overall colour of the plant is green which, combined with its diminutive size – these plants are only about three inches (seven centimetres) high – means that it is very difficult to find. If one looks closely at the

flowers they are as intricate as one would expect from an orchid. The main feature is the helmet-like structure made of petals and sepals over the long lip. The flowers are pollinated by insects which rub against the pollinia when they visit the flowers.

'Over here is an odd-looking plant – carline thistle, *Carlina vulgaris*. It has these hardy straw-coloured inner bracts that give it the appearance of an "everlasting" flower. The specimens along here are very low growing as the turf is so short and they will persist well into the autumn.

'Another plant that is difficult to spot, which should be along here, is the bastard toadflax, *Thesium humifusum*. It has these

pale yellowish-green stems and a very insignificant looking greenish-white flower. Usually you suddenly see some and then realise you've been walking on it. It has a creeping habit like squinancywort but is a rather special plant as, despite its name, it is the only British representative of the more tropical sandalwood family. It is semi-parasitic on other downland herbs and is confined to the chalk and limestone grasslands of southern Britain.

'Changing our perspective for a while we ought to look out for some of the late-flying butterflies as this stretch here is particularly good for them. One day a week in the summer months I do a count of the butterflies on the reserve. It is part of a national survey so I have to decide on a specific walk and when certain factors, such as temperature and sunshine are above an agreed minimum and the wind is below a certain speed, I go out and count every butterfly that I see within a five-metre "corridor". This can then be used as an index to judge the butterfly numbers from one year to the next. We've only seen meadow browns up until now, which is fascinating as only a fortnight ago I counted seventeen species here, last week I saw twelve and by next week it will probably be down to about six. The blustery wind that we have today is undoubtedly keeping a lot of them down.

Making its methodical way across the turf, this bloody-nosed beetle, *Timarcha tenebricosa,* **looks like some extraordinary monster with its segmented legs and glossy black carapace.**

One of the classic butterflies of the chalk downs is the male adonis blue butterfly, *Lysandra bellargus*, seen here resting on a stemless thistle.

'The short turf has several members of the pea-family growing in it, such as horse-shoe vetch, *Hippocrepis comosa*, which is the food plant of two of our classic chalkland butter-flies – the chalkhill blue, *Lysandra coridon*, and the adonis blue, *L. bellargus*. The adult chalkhill blues are on the wing for most of August and should still be around. Although the adonis blue is nationally rather rare, it does breed along here and its second brood should still be flying.'

We had been hoping to see these butterflies since our visit to the South Downs in July, as we had then just missed the earlier June

brood. Paul told us what to look out for.

'The way to tell them apart when you have several species of "blue" in one area is the general colour of the males: in the common blue it is a kind of purpley-blue, while the chalkhill blue is a very pale blue with darker edges and the adonis blue is a very uniform sky blue.'

Encouragingly, a chalkhill blue came fluttering past and landed briefly on a knapweed. Several more flew up as we walked along the dyke, but there was no sign of an adonis blue. Perhaps the wind was keeping them low but suddenly, from the

taller plants in the dyke bottom, a beautiful male flew up and obligingly rested on a nearby stemless thistle. Although it had obviously been around for a while, as its wing edges were frayed, we could clearly see the black veins crossing over its white border, which immediately told it apart from the common blue. The rich azure blue colour of the wings and body was quite unmistakeable – all together an excellent little butterfly. Unlike the chalkhill blue which overwinters as an egg, the caterpillars of the second brood of the adonis blue hibernate over winter and turn into pupae the following spring, to emerge in late May and June. Because the food plant of the caterpillars – the horse-shoe vetch – only grows on this very short downland turf, the management of these areas is crucial if the population is to survive.

Whilst we were looking at this lovely butterfly, Paul found another speciality of the dyke – not a butterfly but a grasshopper this time – the striped-winged grasshopper, *Stenobothus lineatus*. Again, we had heard these on the South Downs but had not seen one. Close-up its colours of green and brown were quite striking. It took a certain degree of skill to catch the grasshoppers as they moved

A striped-winged grasshopper, *Stenobothrus lineatus*, **about to leap to safety from the spikey flower head of a carline thistle.**

Two local chalkland organisms for the price of one! Another adonis blue amongst a creeping mat of bastard toadflax, *Thesium humifusum*, Britain's sole representative of the tropical sandalwood family.

with alarming speed. However, the next insect we came across presented no such problem – this was a bloody-nosed beetle, *Timarcha tenebricosa*. This magnificent glossy black beetle had an amazing defence mechanism, which meant that it didn't need to be fast to evade predators. If it is disturbed it exudes deep red blood from its mouth – hence the name. It is relatively common in grasslands and feeds on bedstraws. It is the largest of our leaf-beetles and can grow up to two centimetres (three-quarters of an inch) in length and is flightless, having no wings and fused elytra. We carefully put the beetle back down and watched it make its way slowly across the turf, seemingly unperturbed at being picked up. We then headed further along the dyke to the area where the down had been ploughed up during the last war. Paul described the scene.

'Although the grassland by the dyke is ranker than further up it is still very old as it has remained intact since the dyke was built. It would have been grazed by sheep up until the last war and then by rabbits until 1954. So the turf has become overgrown with rough grasses only in the last twenty-five years or so. There are still some of the classic chalk downland species here such as the horse-shoe vetch and rock-rose, *Helianthemum chamaecistus*, but if we look just a little way from the dyke we can see that the grassland is very different. This, as we have said, was ploughed up only 25 years ago and although the soils are not very fertile, so there isn't the dense growth of grasses that we had at the start of the walk, the herbs are very noticeably different from those on the older areas. We have a lot of wild carrot and basil, some nice areas with harebells, *Campanula rotundiflora*, rough hawkbit, *Leontodon hispidus*, and burnet-saxifrage, but we don't have the more exacting plants such as the chalk vetches, and the rock-rose, certainly no bastard toadflax or stemless thistle. It will probably take at least another forty years with careful management before it has the richness of some of the older grassland. However, some plants are here: there are orchids coming in already such as the pyramidal orchid, *Anacamptis pyramidalis*, and the spotted orchid, *Dactylorizha fuchsii*. The dominant grass is *Arrhenatherum elatius*, false oat-grass. Another interesting thing to notice is that there does seem to be an element of luck as to the species composition in each patch. For instance, over here is a reasonable amount of eyebright, *Euphrasia*,

in the community, but further down you will notice that it is totally absent. This whole area is being grazed hard at the moment to keep the turf as open as possible, but it all takes time. We are very lucky here, as there is a reserve of plants that can gradually colonise the ground but in the vast majority of cases the areas of chalk downland are so small and fragmented that once they have been "improved" by fertilizers and reseeded or ploughed, they are lost forever. One has only to look at the decrease in chalk downland since the war to realise how true this is.'

As we walked back towards the cars, small groups of swallows and house martins were sweeping across the down picking off the insects in the late afternoon sun. They would soon be gathering to migrate southwards. Some of the grasses had already turned a light straw colour, reminding us that autumn was just around the corner. But Paul had a full schedule of work mapped out for the winter so that the flowers would hopefully be even better next summer. We had only seen a small fragment of the rich wildlife of our chalk downs but it was enough to know that they were more than worth preserving for the future and certainly exciting enough to fill any walk with interest and colour.

A traditional sign of autumn along the chalk downs and ways – the long plumed fruits of traveller's joy, *Clematis vitalba.*

A northern grassland walk

Malham Cove is one of the great wonders of natural Britain and certainly one of the highlights of the Pennine Way. It is a place in which you can really get the feel of the power which creates landscapes. It would never surprise me if, on arriving at the top, you found a glacier still in position eroding the rock away! Trevor Elkington not only knows the place but its plants as well. Brought up in David Valentine's school of experimental taxonomy at Durham, he records variety where most of us see uniformity and understands how those minute differences between the individuals of each population are moulded by environment and chance into new species. Here he takes on his other role as an ecologist and explains the interplay between environment and vegetation; and how the intermix of limestone, glacial drift and past land-use provides a patchwork of diversity.

The towering limestone cliffs of Malham Cove, perhaps one of the most spectacular views along the Pennine Way.

Information

Many naturalists consider the chalk hills of southern Britain to be the best places to explore the plants and insects that inhabit these basic soils. However, the northern limestone grasslands have their own specialities and the hard Carboniferous Limestones have produced some spectacular landscapes, such as at Ingleborough and Malham in Yorkshire, with their steep exposed cliff faces and rock strewn plateaux.

A further feature which makes these areas of particular interest are the limestone pavements.

These are areas which are dominated by blocks of limestone rock which have been exposed by glacial action and subsequently eroded, over thousands of years, by rainwater which has dissolved the limestone along the natural joints creating the pavement effect that can be seen today.

The grykes provide a fascinating habitat for an interesting group of plants, many of which would appear to be more at home in a woodland setting. However, the conditions in the deeper grykes are not that dissimilar to those that could be found on a woodland floor.

Formation of a limestone pavement

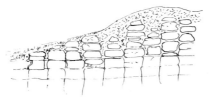

Cross-section of section of area
of limestone
showing top soil
and weathered limestone before glaciation

Same area soon after top layers
have been removed by movement
of ice during glaciation

Same area today where the natural
joints in the limestone have been
opened out by the action of rain

Plants to look out for in limestone pavements

male fern *Dryopteris filix-mas*
hard shield fern *Polystichum aculeatum*
hart's tongue fern *Phyllitis scolopendrium*
wall spleenwort *Asplenium ruta-muraria*
maidenhair spleenwort *Asplenium trichomanes*
limestone polypody *Thylypteris robertiana*
baneberry *Actaea spicata*
herb robert *Geranium robertianum*
upright red currant *Ribes spicatum*
bloody cranesbill *Geranium sanguineum*
dog's mercury *Mercurialis perennis*
dog violet *Viola riviniana*
lily-of-the-valley *Convallaria majalis*
angular solomon's seal *Polygonatum odoratum*

Some typical plants of northern grasslands

The traditional hay-meadows of some northern areas contain a rich diversity of plants which are often very different from those that are found in southern England. These might include melancholy thistle, globe flower and wood cranesbill. Wetter areas of grassland might include the delightful bird's-eye primrose and grass of parnassus.

globe flower *Trollius europaeus*
spring sandwort *Minuartia verna*
wood cranesbill *Geranium sylvaticum*
bloody cranesbill *Geranium sanguineum*
grass of parnassus *Parnassia palustris*
bird's-eye primrose *Primula farinosa*
giant bellflower *Campanula latifolia*
lady's mantle *Alchemilla vulgaris*
mountain pansy *Viola lutea*
mountain everlasting *Antennaria dioica*
melancholy thistle *Cirsium heterophyllum*
blue moor grass *Sesleria caerulea*

Sites

Upper Teesdale, Durham. Visitor centre for area at Bowlees, Newbiggin. Outstanding region for upland flora with traditional haymeadows in some regions. Nature trails.
Humphrey Head, Lancashire. A limestone headland in Morecambe Bay with a rich variety of flowers and splendid views across the bay.
Orton Meadows, Cumbria. Hay meadows and grazed grassland on limestone soils. Rich in plant species such as bird's-eye primrose.
Hutton Roof, Cumbria. A limestone pavement covering an extensive area with many characteristic species.
Ingleborough, Yorkshire. A famous peak in the Pennine chain with spectacular limestone scenery including caves. There are large areas of limestone pavement including an RSNC reserve at Southerscales Scar, Chapel-le-Dale, which has good limestone grassland and typical pavement flora.
Malham, Yorkshire. This popular area of the Yorkshire Dales has a wide range of Carboniferous Limestone features including scree slopes, limestone pavement and cliffs at Malham Cove. See overleaf for further details.
Derbyshire Dales. This area contains the southern-most limit for many of the northern plants such as the globe flower and melancholy thistle. There are many excellent walks using Matlock as a centre.
Great Ormes Head, Caernarvonshire. A famous high limestone headland with a fascinating variety of maritime and limestone plants growing on its steep slopes, including many rare species.
The Burren, Country Clare. A vast area of limestone pavements of international importance. Contains a rich diversity of plants including many rare arctic-alpine and Mediterranean plants such as mountain avens and maidenhair fern.

A northern grassland walk
with
Trevor Elkington

Britain, despite its comparatively small size, is a land full of visual contrasts. One day you can be admiring the gentle rolling scenery of the Downs and the next clambering across the craggy Pennine uplands. Essentially both types of landscape can be called grasslands and, although it is more usual to associate the broad lowland valleys or southern hills with open grassy swards, the dramatic scenery of the Yorkshire Dales has as much to offer and just as old a tale to tell. When we went up for a day in the Dales we found that it also had some surprises that were every bit as intriguing as could be found anywhere in Britain.

For sheer spectacle the landscape around Malham, in the Yorkshire Dales National Park, is hard to beat and yet with the guidance of our expert for the day, Dr Trevor Elkington, we discovered that there was more than one way of looking at the view. Trevor is a senior lecturer in botany at Sheffield University and has a special interest in the plant ecology of Britain's grasslands. We met in the village of Malham which nowadays is a busy tourist trap during the summer months, complete with a well-kept interpretive centre showing the many interesting walks that can be taken from the village. Trevor was keen to show us around the Cove, so having kitted up ready for a typical summer's day of sun and showers, we headed out north of the village to join part of the famous Pennine Way. Before long we were off the road and looking out across what must be one of the most exciting views along the footpath – Malham Cove. The cliffs of the Cove were towering out of the green rock-strewn landscape right ahead of us. Whilst we surveyed this impressive view we asked Trevor to tell us something of the background to the area.

'Today we are at Malham in the North Pennines which form part of the ridge of hills which runs north from the Peak District in Derbyshire to the Scottish Border. In particular we are in the Craven region of North Yorkshire. The origin of the word "craven" is not that clear but some people say that it is derived from the same word as "crag", meaning rocky, and obviously that would make sense as everywhere we look around here there are rocks.

'We've just walked up through Malham village and in front of us are the cliffs of Malham Cove which rise in a sheer wall of about 300 feet (90 metres). As we look across the landscape on either side of the Cove we can see that there is a great ridge of hills

running across in front of us. They are the result of a very ancient fracture in the Earth's surface known as the Mid-Craven Fault. Basically, the ground we are on has moved down several hundred feet while the block to the north of us has remained stable. The exposed rock that we can see is Carboniferous Limestone, which was formed roughly at the same time as the coals, some 300 million years ago. Whereas the coal was formed in swamps and consists largely of plant remains, the limestone was formed in shallow tropical seas and is largely composed of skeletal remains of many sea creatures. It has, of course, been exposed to very different types of climate since that period. This limestone is a great deal harder than the chalk of Southern England, producing a much more rugged scenery. The specific Carboniferous Limestone here is known as the Great Scar Limestone; it is one of the thickest bands of limestone in the Pennines – over 500 feet (160 metres) deep. The hills to the north of this have younger rocks on top of this limestone – the so-called Yoredale series – which consists of bands of limestone, shale and sandstone with some bands of coal. In fact, one of the hills has coal seams near its summit at over 2000 feet (620 metres), which were mined in the last century. The limestone also contains veins of lead and zinc ores which were both mined in the past. This is the broad geological background to the area although, as we will see later on, the surface of the land has been considerably affected by glaciation.

'The history of human settlement in the area goes back a surprisingly long way and there are obvious features which point to the various stages in the settlement of the dale. There is evidence that Mesolithic man hunted in this region some thousands of years ago. These people were hunter gatherers who ranged widely across the upland area. They were followed by Neolithic people, probably the first settlers of the area. In turn these were replaced by the Bronze Age people who have left visible signs of their presence to this day in the shape of standing stones, the nearest being about three miles from Malham village. The most extensive remains of prehistoric man belong to the people of the Iron Age living here in the centuries before the Roman invasion and cultivating small, walled fields as well as keeping cattle and sheep.

'The fact that we can still see many surface remains from this period also suggests that

A view of the ancient landscape around Malham – pastures studded with flowers and transected by stone walls.

the original forest cover would have already been cleared by this time. The Romans had very little impact on the region, leaving it more or less as a "native reservation". After they left there was a continuation of the settlement of the dale. On the hillside opposite we can see banks or terraces running across the slope. These are lynchets – strips of land which were regularly ploughed by teams of oxen – dating from the Dark Ages. Within a hundred years of the Norman Conquest most of the land had been given or sold to the monasteries, such as Fountains Abbey to the east and Bolton Priory to the west. The region then became monastic land for the next 300 to 400 years up until the Dissolution. Both the monasteries used the land for sheep farming, and by and large this use of the land continues through to the present day.

'The stone walls that we can see date from several periods. The lynchets, originally each owned individually, were probably used right through to the eighteenth century and were then swapped and sold to consolidate them into small, walled fields. The walls that run right across the hillsides are later, dating from the Enclosure Acts, and were mostly built in the course of the last century. Therefore we can now appreciate that since the clearing of the forests most of the area has been grazed by sheep, producing the closely cropped grassy landscape that we can see today. Just how important these sheep are, we will see further on.'

We moved off along the path towards the Cove but were soon distracted by large numbers of thistles and clumps of nettles growing in the field. Why was this? Surely they are unpalatable to the sheep; hardly the product of hundreds of years of sheep-rearing husbandry. We asked Trevor what they indicated.

'These show the effects of fertilizers on this type of grassland. Nettle is a plant which requires high levels of nutrients in the soil whereas natural limestone grassland has very few nutrients, particularly nitrogen and phosphorus, which, as every gardener knows, are essential for the vigorous growth of plants. So their presence here indicates that the farmer has added something to the ground. The large numbers of thistles indicate disturbance as well. This is creeping thistle, *Cirsium arvense*, which is not a plant naturally found in a limestone grassland community. But it is a fast growing plant with numerous underground creeping stems which are very difficult to eradicate.

'The native limestone plants have low rates of growth so they are adapted to the usually low levels of nutrients present in the

Sheep, like these, have been grazing these hills for hundreds of years producing a finely cropped turf. Where the farmer has upset the balance by adding fertilizers or where the ground has been disturbed, invasive weeds like these thistles, *Cirsium arvense,* **can become dominant.**

soil. If artificial fertilizers are put on the grass the immediate effect is to encourage the vigorous coarse-leaved grasses with high rates of growth – plants such as false oat-grass, *Arrhenatherum elatius*, cocks-foot, *Dactylis glomerata* and here, tufted hair-grass *Deschampsia cespitosa*. These grasses tend to form a very dense community and shade out the very low growing herbs and grasses, so the net result is a much less diverse grassland with few species in it. If there is a degree of disturbance as well then invasive plants like these nettles and thistles will move in.'

We walked on past this veritable forest of thistles to some fields nearer to the base of the Cove. At first glance these looked no different to the one we had just gone through, except the nettles and thistles had gone. However, Trevor knew better and knelt down by a low hummock to show us some of the plants.

'Well, we've now gone on to the next field and if we look a bit higher up this one we can see a line of stones running across the hillside. That is, in fact, the remains of an Iron Age stone wall and to the right of it are known to be the remains of hut circles from the same period. So here we have the original site of a settlement and the fact that these remains are still here indicates that this particular grassland has not been disturbed for at least 2000 years. If we look at the turf we can see it is a very intricate mixture of species; indeed some of these grasslands can have forty or more different plants in a square metre. The grasses are now just coming into flower. Here we have the most common in this area, with its very fine leaves – sheep's fescue, *Festuca ovina*. Then we have the grass with quaking heads, quaking or totter grass, *Briza media*. Another common grass here that is flowering is crested dogs-tail grass, *Cynosurus cristatus*.'

Trevor then crouched even closer to the ground and I am sure would have got down on his stomach if it hadn't been raining. We followed his gaze as he surveyed this minia-ture world of flowers oblivious of the loom-ing cliffs of the Cove above us.

'If we get a bit closer to the ground we can see that one of the commonest plants flower-ing around us is Wild Thyme, *Thymus praecox*. Then there are some white flowers of the clover *Trifolium repens*. If we come a little closer still to the ground we can see the small trifoliate leaves of birds-foot trefoil, *Lotus corniculatus*, and then the pinnate

leaves of salad burnet, *Poterium sanguisorba*. Unfortunately, most of the flowering shoots have been eaten off by the sheep. However, if we look across the grass we can see one or two pale yellow daisy-like flowers. These belong to *Pilosella officinarum*, a member of the Composite family of flowers. Right down amongst the leaves you can just see the very fine dissected leaves of yarrow, *Achillea millefolium* and those of lady's bed-straw, *Galium verum*. If we were to look around we'd find several more that we could distin-guish. But even so you can see it is a rich community of species. The high diversity ironically depends on the low nutrient levels and if we started to apply fertilizers to this, as we saw just now, we would lose many of the plants.'

Trevor got up off his knees. Perhaps the walkers on the Pennine Way thought we were some strange sect paying homage to the Cove. But there is no substitute for really getting down and studying the plants, feeling their shapes and taking in the rich scents. Just cruising along trying to keep up a steady average walking speed is a good way of reaching your destination but you'll miss almost as much as you'll see. The sun had come out now and we sat down for a while as Trevor told us some more about the intricate ecology of the grassland.

The flowerhead of a very common plant of limestone and chalk grasslands – salad burnet, *Poterium sanguisorba*. The tightly packed greenish flowers at the top are usually female with conspicuous reddish stigmas which are branched to catch the wind-blown pollen. They open first, as shown here, to ensure they are pollinated by other plants.

'It's quite interesting to look at the growth cycle of this type of grassland. Obviously it is an evergreen community; we more or less take that for granted. We don't think about it as losing all its leaves like trees in winter, but that is not to say that all the plants in it are evergreen. The purging flax, *Linum catharticum*, with tiny white flowers, is an annual which dies in the autumn. The salad burnet, although a perennial, loses its leaves every autumn and produces a new crop in the spring. Most of the plants have a peak growth in the summer, usually about June or July, but some, such as the rock rose, *Helianthemum chamaecistus*, have a very even growth pattern and it more or less grows at the same rate at which it loses leaves. If we look between the herbs we can also see there are some mosses; they are not very obvious at this time of year but if we came in spring or autumn we would find they were much more important components in the grassland, particularly in the damper north facing slopes. So it is a community which changes in detail from season to season.

'Another interesting part of the biology of these plants is the ways in which they are pollinated. The grasses are all pollinated by the wind and if we look carefully we can see quite obvious stamens which hang out of the flowers releasing large amounts of pollen. They also have large stigmas which catch the pollen as it is blown around in the wind. Some of the herbs are also wind pollinated, salad burnet, for example, has fairly conspicuous reddish stigmas which are branched to catch the pollen. In this plant the flowers at the top of the flower head are normally purely female, those in the middle are hermaphrodite, having both large stamens producing pollen and ovaries forming seed, while the flowers at the base only have stamens and are thus purely male. Generally the female flowers at the top open first so they will tend to be cross-pollinated by pollen blown from other plants, whereas the hermaphrodite flowers lower down may be self- or cross-pollinated. However, most of the herbs in the turf, such as thyme and clover, are insect pollinated and on a sunny day you could sit here and watch quite a number of bees busily moving from one plant to the next. Thyme has open flowers so that they are easily visited and the pollen can be removed successfully by the bees. Plants like clover have a more complex structure which ensures that when the insect lands on the flower the pollen is deposited on its body.

'Over there is a plant which we've not mentioned yet but is very typical of limestone grassland – eyebright, *Euphrasia officinalis*. It has these rather pretty white flowers with conspicuous lines on the corolla and a yellow patch in the centre. The lines act as guides to the visiting insect and direct it toward the nectar and pollen. Eyebright is an interesting plant in its own right. It is an annual which is semi-parasitic, although it has obviously green leaves so it can photosynthesise for itself. Its roots, however, have been shown to link onto other plant roots, particularly grasses, and it then derives some of its food from "stealing" sap from these plants. It has little suckers which actually grow through and into the roots of these other plants.

Opposite **Bulbous buttercups,** *Ranunculus bulbosus*, **a typical plant of dry calcareous grassland, with some red clover,** *Trifolium pratense*.

Above **An area fenced off from the sheep. Here the grasses are able to flower uncropped. The distinctive flowering panicles of crested dog's-tail** *Cynosurus cristatus* **and cocksfoot,** *Dactylis glomeratus*, **can be seen.**

Above **A view of the open ashwoods of the Dale. These woods, which have probably been left because of their inaccessible position, were originally the dominant cover of the dales before the arrival of man.**

Opposite top **Mosses and maidenhair spleenwort,** *Asplenium trichomanes,* **growing in a rock crevice at the bottom of the Cove.**

Opposite bottom **Thyme,** *Thymus praecox,* **and fescue grass growing in a miniature rock garden on thin soils amongst the limestone.**

'Before we move on there is one other flower I should show you – a buttercup. Now, many people think they are all the same but in fact there are several species of buttercups. This particular one is typical of limestone and chalk grassland. If I just remove some of the turf from around its base we can see that it has a corm rather like a small *Crocus*. In the autumn it dies back to this corm which acts as a food reserve for the winter. In the spring it puts out new leaves then later in the summer it flowers. This bulb-like structure, which is absent in the other buttercups, gives it its name – bulbous buttercup, *Ranunculus bulbosus*. An easier way of identifying it is to look underneath the flower where you can see that the greenish sepals are turned back against the stem, while in the other species they clasp the flower.'

Before we went off to look at the crags, Trevor took us over to a fenced area by the path. It had been cordoned off as it had been severely eroded when the original path went through it. The National Park Authority has now built a completely new path which is much more resistant to the thousands of feet which pass along it each year. As we looked over the fence Trevor explained what was happening to the vegetation.

'This enclosed area is interesting from a botanical point of view as it shows us what happens when sheep are removed from an area of grassland. The first thing you can see is that all the grasses are flowering here, whereas when we were out on the open pasture it was difficult to find individual flowering heads. This has not been fenced off for long and so the species composition is similar to that outside, but already we can see the bunchy flower heads of cocks-foot grass becoming conspicuous. As time goes on, these coarser-leaved grasses will increase and the plants themselves and their decaying litter will eventually shade out the smaller herbs.

'Another important factor that we can see here is the trees. The young ash saplings have been planted and the intention is to turn this into a wooded area. They have also planted some hawthorns but these would almost certainly have come in naturally, given time. We have already seen several old hawthorns growing on the slopes and if you took the sheep away these would produce seedlings, and over the years a dense scrub of hawthorn would develop and the grassland would be shaded out. In time you might find ash becoming established, protected by the hawthorn scrub, and a new ash wood would begin. So this grassland that is all around us is really an artificial community dependent on grazing.'

This was all rather salutory but how did the landscape develop from bare rock to a

93

rich grassy sward? A careful examination of some of the limestone outcrops provided part of the answer. Trevor found a nearby crag with what looked like a miniature rock garden growing along its edges and showed us just what was gradually happening to the rockface.

'We've come to some low crags to see how the limestone grassland develops from the original rock. The rock itself is a patchwork of whites and greys with some rather greenish patches. These are all lichens which are partially growing within the rock itself. As they develop over the years they produce small amounts of humus from the decaying parts and in time this humus washes into cracks and is colonised by mosses. In turn the mosses will produce decaying matter and give us the first soil in which flowering plants can root. We can see that in the crevices there

Right **Where the soils are deeper a more varied community of plants can develop. Here is a colourful mixture of thyme, bedstraws and herb robert,** *Geranium robertianum.*

Opposite **On the more exposed crags can be found the highly adaptable harebell,** *Campanula rotundiflora.* **Quite often these crags are carpeted with a hair-moss called** *Rhacomitrum lanuginosum.*

Opposite **A view out across the limestone pavement at the top of the Cove. This remarkable landscape is produced by a combination of glacial erosion of the original weathered top soil and the effect of rain over many thousands of years.**

are plants like thyme and some fescue rooting and producing a slightly deeper soil. If we look at the soil itself it is rather crumbly and black with very little mineral matter in it. Interestingly, in some pockets where you have this dark crumbly soil it is almost completely formed from the droppings of small animals, particularly minute insects called springtails. Eventually, it will be colonised by plants and a deeper soil will form and after a long while a closed grassland will develop. All this shallow grassland

sward around here would probably have started like that. However, when we get onto the general pasture we also have to consider the effects of glaciation as some of the deeper soils will include glacial drift.

'If we look around the crag we can see that it has been colonised by several sorts of plants. Firstly, in the crevices where there is a lot of moisture there are some nice clumps of mosses. Further down also in the crevices and fissures are two ferns. This one is maidenhair spleenwort, *Asplenium tricho-*

Left **The grykes or gullies between the blocks of limestone make a highly unusual habitat for many plants that might normally be found in a woodland environment. Here can be seen the fronds of male fern,** *Dryopteris filix-mas,* **amongst dog's mercury,** *Mercurialis perennis,* **ash,** *Fraxinus excelsior,* **and stinging nettle,** *Urtica dioica.*

manes, which has these green "leaflets" and a black stem or rachis, as they are called in ferns. The other one is wall rue, *Asplenium ruta-muraria*, which is closely related to the spleenwort. They grow in these damp crevices, not because the adult plants that we see here need that much moisture, but more because the first stage in their life cycle is very sensitive to drying.'

We now moved on up the path that skirted the edge of the Cove. From here we had a splendid view of the ash wood on the opposite slope. That side was a great deal steeper and between the trees the ground was covered with broken fragments of rock. It is probable that the wood has never been completely clear felled and therefore stands as a reminder of a landscape that has largely disappeared over 2000 years ago. Meanwhile, Trevor had located some nearby crags which were out of reach of the sheep and so we went over to investigate.

'We are standing up against some taller crags which the sheep have clearly been unable to reach as we can see a much taller community of plants. It also contains some rather different species. One grass here that is quite interesting is blue sesleria or blue moor-grass, *Sesleria caerulea*. This is a plant of northern limestone which reaches its southern limit in Britain in this region. It flowers early in the spring and has a blue-tinted flowering head. Later in the year it is still fairly easy to pick out as it has fairly broad leaves with boat-shaped tips. Definitely a plant to look out for when you are in northern limestone grasslands. We also have some of the grasses we saw on the pasture but growing a good deal taller here due to the absence of grazing. A common plant of the crags and scree slopes, as well as being a typical woodland flower is Herb Robert, *Geranium robertianum*. It is one of the fairly small group of plants which has two quite distinct habitats. It is very easily picked out by its reddish stems, divided leaves and typical geranium fruiting structures, which give the group their other name of crane's-bills. The other plant in flower on the crag here is Harebell, *Campanula rotundifolia*, the "bluebell" of Scotland. This familiar plant is found in a wide variety of habitats and is highly successful at obtaining a root-hold in these crevices. Carpeting the surface of the rock just here is a distinctive moss covered with very long white hairs, giving it a rather greyish appearance. It is called woolly hair-moss, a plant which has the long scientific name of *Rhacomitrium lanuginosum*. Again, like the *Sesleria* it has a northern distribution. It is essentially a mountain plant and if you go to the Lake District or the mountains of Wales or Scotland you will find great sheets of this over the rocks. And again, like our lower crag, if you look closely at the rocky surface you will see that almost all of it is covered with various lichens.'

We then climbed our way towards the top of the Cove. As we ascended the steps of the path the view behind us gradually opened out into a vista of greens broken by clumps of sycamore and ash linked by an intricate maze of stone walls. Once out on the plateau at the top of the Cove we were immediately struck by the strange landscape of flat, bare rock cut through with numerous channels. Trevor knew this formation well and described it to us.

'We are standing at the top of Malham Cove and are looking across at a classic example of a rock formation known as limestone pavement. As the name implies it is a very rough pavement of blocks of limestone with cracks in between. Interestingly the words that describe the features of the pavement are old Yorkshire dialect words. The blocks are called "clints" and the cracks which divide them are called "grykes". Some of the grykes here are, in fact, quite deep, up to six feet (two metres) or more in depth.

'This is a formation which one certainly does not see in all parts of the country where there is limestone. For example, in the Peak District to the south there is a great deal of Carboniferous limestone but no pavements. Why is this? Well, to explain it we have to go back to the glacial periods. What most people think of as the glacial period, in fact, was a sequence of at least four glaciations with long warm periods in between them. The last of these, the Devensian glaciation, ended about

12000 years ago, and was not as widespread as the others, one of which at least covered the Midlands. The Devensian glaciation had a major centre of ice formation in the Lake District and from there the ice spread out to the south and east and completely covered the Malham area.

'If we look to the south we can see a low valley running across from east to west in front of us. This is the valley of the River Aire, the so-called Aire gap, which separates the northern part of the Pennines from the uplands further south. The ice is thought to have spread out in this valley with one tongue going west towards present day Lancashire and the other to the east towards the Vale of York. Further south there was no continuous ice covering of the countryside. The importance of this is that the grinding action and weight of the moving ice scraped away the old weathered rock in this region, exposing fresh limestone. Further south in the Derby-

Herb robert growing amongst the limestone pavement. This plant grows in a wide variety of sites from southern woodlands to mountain crags and is obviously flourishing in these grykes.

shire Peak District this process did not take place, so that, except on very steep slopes, there is a covering of weathered rock and a substantial depth of soil. Another important result of the glaciation was deposition of glacial drift, consisting of masses of soil, rocks, boulders and clay. This was deposited by the retreated glaciers in a fairly indiscriminate fashion across the landscape. If you were to excavate a pavement that is still beneath the drift you would find that the pattern of the clints is much more regular than in exposed sections and that the grykes are not very open. On the exposed areas erosion by water has made these cracks much more prominent. The action of running water is itself an erosive force, but the other major way that erosion has taken place is through solution. As it rains the water passing through the air picks up carbon dioxide and becomes a very weak acid. The limestone is very pure, in fact it is 99·5% calcium carbonate, which means that if you dissolve it only 0·5% would remain as a solid. So this weak acidic liquid falling over thousands of years is slowly dissolving the limestone and gradually widening and deepening the cracks. We can also see that the limestone has runnels in it and again these were formed by the water running along slopes in the limestone and dissolving it away. One might ask why you do not get similar pavements on other types of rock. The reason seems to be that if you have a fairly soft rock like a shale, then the ice grinds this down to the same slope as the ice itself, whereas the limestone, which is a much harder rock, was resistant to the ice flow and only the weathered part was removed.

'If we look at the pavement in detail, we can see that towards the edge, where it probably has always been exposed, the blocks are quite solid and regular. If we look back to where it is emerging from the grassland the pavement is much more irregular. What seems to have happened here is that this section of the pavement was at one time underneath a thin layer of drift. This forms a rather acidic soil, so the water percolating down to the rock below became more acid, resulting in more solution of the limestone taking place underneath the drift than where the rock has been exposed for the whole of the post-glacial period.

'If we look across the surface of the pavement we can see very few plants at all. However, if we look down into the grykes we find that they are actually full of plants.

Strangely, considering that we are standing on a very exposed upland area, if we look at the plants we find that many of them are species which are commonly found in woodlands. For example, in front of us we have a gryke full of dog's mercury, *Mercurialis perennis*, with a healthy specimen of male fern, *Dryopteris filix-mas*, growing up in between them. If we walk over here we can see in the deeper grykes some lovely hart's-tongue fern, *Phyllitis scolopendrium*, with their distinctive strap-like leathery fronds. There is also some maidenhair spleenwort. There are some more areas with the familiar herb robert which is certainly a woodland plant although, as we have noted, it will also grow on ungrazed rock ledges. All rather surprising. But if we think about the micro-environment that these plants are living in there is a logic here. Firstly, the grykes are protected from the worst of the weather, they have a fairly high humidity and, of course, are quite shaded, at least in the deeper areas; all of which reflect the conditions of a woodland environment. The other possible reason why we have woodland plants here is that originally this was, indeed, woodland. Now today, we do not see any trees on the

The yellow flower and tightly bunched fleshy leaves of biting stone-crop, *Sedum acre*, growing in one of the shallower grykes of the pavement.

Arum maculatum, a characteristic woodland plant but very much at home in the grykes. Also, amongst these were the distinctive heart-shaped leaves of the dog violet, *Viola riviniana*. There were also some further woodland ferns such as the delicate brittle bladder fern, *Cystopteris fragilis*, a plant with essentially a northern distribution.

Having looked at this most unusual collection of plants we made our way across to an area of grassland on the northern edge of the pavement. The grassland here was quite different to anything we had seen so far. Trevor showed us some of the plants that indicated this.

'Here we've just walked to the back of the limestone pavement and despite being only a short distance from the solid bed rock we are now on a quite different type of grassland. This is characterised by species which favour much more acid conditions. This is essentially because we are now on drift soil which is not derived from the limestone, but was brought in by ice action from further north. If we look at the turf we can see some typical grasses of acid turf. First of all we have *Anthoxanthum odoratum*, sweet vernal grass, which is quite a common grass of soils of moderate acidity. Over here we have bent grass, *Agrostis tenuis*, again characteristic of acid soils. There are also some distinctive herbs such as heath bedstraw *Galium saxatile* and tormentil, *Potentilla erecta*, both of which contrast markedly with the lime-loving plants we have seen up until now. Finally to underline this, here is some sheep's sorrel, *Rumex acetosella*, with its distinctive hastate leaves which look rather like a miniature medieval lance and if you chew them they taste slightly bitter owing to their acidity.'

We turned back to look at the pavement and found that a large group of students, probably from the field centre at Malham Tarn, were making their way uneasily across the clints, their brightly coloured anoraks contrasting vividly with the cold grey of the rock. Unfortunately, not many of them looked down to see the intricate rock gardens almost beneath their feet, but looked instead beyond the Cove at the great sweep of the dale. Both worlds were visually stunning and both were intimately bound up with each other as we now knew. So next time you go out for a ramble amongst the beauty of the dales, like Trevor, have a closer look at the grasses and flowers and, perhaps, you will discover that there is even more to the richness of the landscape.

Usually found growing in shady hedgebanks and woods, this hart's tongue fern, *Phyllitis scolopendrium*, seems quite at home in the shade of this deep gryke.

pavement although there are some ashes on the crags below. However, if we look around we can find some hawthorns and ashes which have been browsed off as they have come to the top of the clint. So there are indications that this was probably wooded in the past. We can actually see this situation about ten miles further north where there is an ash-wood on the limestone pavement, with similar plants to here growing in the grykes.'

We then made our way across the pavement. Fortunately, it had now stopped raining and the brisk wind had more or less dried the surface. However, we still had to tread very carefully. Our searches soon produced some more plants. One in particular was *Actaea spicata*, an extremely poisonous relative of the buttercups, with the suitably off-putting common name of bane-berry. Although widespread in northern Europe, in Britain it is more or less restricted to these areas of limestone ashwoods and pavements in northern England. The plant has distinctive toothed trifoliate leaves, with a head of small white flowers. Later in the year it carries shiny black poisonous berries.

Another plant that we soon discovered was the familiar cuckoo-pint or lords and ladies,

A meadow walk

Francis Rose is not only one of the greatest field botanists alive today but is one of the greatest that has ever lived. He was the man who, to use the modern jargon, 'turned me on' to the world of plants. He was also my research director and, whilst I studied for my PhD, I had the privilege of walking and talking with him during the five most formative years of my career. This chapter brings you one afternoon of that magic as he takes you on a walk through one of the most magical of all types of grassland, the water meadow. In the days before the use and abuse of fertilizers, water meadows were of great importance to the local economy. The upland fields had to be manured or the crops rotated, in order to maintain fertility. Not so the water meadows, as in most winters they received a new supply of nutrient rich silts, absolutely free, from the river flood waters. They were ideal places to reap one or more good crops of herb-rich hay to dry for winter feed. It was this age-old management practice which helped to make and maintain our water meadows as sanctuaries for a great diversity of plants and birds. Perhaps, with the rising cost of chemical fertilizers, they will once again become economic entities in our river-scapes; until then, we will have to work to preserve the few that still remain.

A splendid view from the river across a large stretch of traditional wet meadowland. The apparently flat nature of the land is misleading as it is transected by numerous ditches and channels. Furthermore, the tussocky nature of the vegetation makes walking a slow but rewarding business.

Information

Traditional water meadows and hay meadows

Of all the major habitat types that are threatened, the traditional species-rich water meadows and hay meadows of lowland Britain are the ones most at risk. This is because they are essentially the product of a type of farming that is no longer practiced. At one time, the areas of grassland in the broad alluvial plains of lowland rivers were considered prize agricultural land. Their importance resulted from the problems of feeding livestock during the winter months. These wet meadows could be flooded in late winter, which not only replenished the fertility of the soil, but also protected the ground from late frosts, allowing the grass to shoot earlier in the year than on neighbouring land. Today, however, these areas are somewhat of an anachronism as imported foodstuffs and chemical fertilizers have largely obviated the need for the more traditional methods. Also, the current emphasis on cereal crops, which are heavily subsidised, means that the modern farmer is more likely to drain these areas and turn his production over to arable farming. The Water Authorities assist the farmers in carrying out these large scale drainage schemes with support from the Ministry of Agriculture. Furthermore, where meadows have remained, many of them have changed in a more subtle way, as they have probably been heavily fertilized or reseeded with rye-grass and clover which has just as devastating an effect on the traditional species composition. Some of the remaining meadows have histories of similar management going back over many centuries. This continuity of management has often been sustained as the meadows were either jointly owned or common land, being grazed during the autumn and winter and laid-up for hay in the spring and early summer.

Plants which are indicators of traditional species-rich meadows:

adder's tongue fern *Ophioglossum vulgatum*
common meadow-rue *Thalictrum flavum*
great burnet *Sanguisorba officinalis*
meadow saxifrage *Saxifraga granulata*
cowslip *Primula veris*
pepper-saxifrage *Silaum silaus*
dyer's greenweed *Genista tinctora*
yellow rattle *Rhinanthus minor*
fritillary *Fritillaria meleagris*
autumn crocus *Colchicum autumnale*
green-winged orchid *Orchis morio*
greater butterfly orchid *Platanthera chlorantha*

Often the feature which immediately brings a traditional meadow to ones attention is the sheer variety of plants, particularly the presence of many types of grass. In wetter areas the following species might also be present:

ragged robin *Lychnis flos-cuculi*
lady's smock *Cardamine pratensis*
water avens *Geum rivale*
marsh thistle *Cirsium palustre*
meadow thistle *Cirsium dissectum*
marsh valerian *Valeriana dioica*
creeping buttercup *Ranunculus repens*
betony *Betonica officinalis*
common spotted orchid *Dactylorhiza fuchsii*
marsh helleborine *Epipactis palustris*
jointed rush *Juncus articulatus*
hard rush *Juncus inflexus*
soft rush *Juncus effusus*
common sedge *Carex nigra*

Birds

Wet meadows, particularly those which flood in the winter, are particularly good for both wintering and breeding birds. The following is a selection of some possible species to look out for:

heron *Ardea cinerea*
Bewick's swan *Cygnus columbianus*
Canada goose *Branta canadensis*
white-fronted goose *Anser albifrons*
bean goose *Anser fabalis*
pink-footed goose *Anser brachyrhynchus*
wigeon *Anas penelope*
teal *Anas crecca*
garganey *Anas querquedula*
mallard *Anas platyrhynchos*
shoveler *Anas clypeata*
moorhen *Gallinula chloropus*
lapwing *Vanellus vanellus*
golden plover *Pluvialis apricaria*
snipe *Gallinago gallinago*
redshank *Tringa totanus*
meadow pipit *Anthus pratensis*
skylark *Alauda arvensis*
yellow wagtail *Motacilla flava*
reed bunting *Emberiza schoeniclus*

Sites

There are very few areas that have extensive traditional meadowland. Often, however, there are small fields which for various reasons have escaped improvement. In recent surveys patches of this type of meadow have been found in such diverse places as churchyards, pony paddocks and orchards. Certain plants such as the fritilliary, which is only found in these habitats, has dramatically decreased in numbers and is now found in only a few widely scattered sites such as in the upper Thames valley in Wiltshire where there are some fine series of water meadows. Other areas that have water meadows are the Somerset Levels, which cover a large area in central Somerset. These levels are flooded in winter providing good wintering conditions for waterfowl such as Bewick's swans and geese and breeding areas in the spring for snipe, redshank and lapwing. They have a rich grassland flora as well. The meadows in the flood plain of the River Arun at Amberley and Waltham and the River Cuckmere in Sussex are very good for both wintering wildfowl and summer meadow plants. The Ouse Washes in Cambridgeshire is justly famous for its wintering wildfowl, including large numbers of Bewick's swans and wigeon and also its nesting waders and ducks. It is also very good for wet pasture flowers. A particularly important stretch is owned as a reserve by the Cambridgeshire and Isle of Ely Naturalists' Trust at Manea.

A meadow walk
with
Francis Rose

When out walking by one of our many lowland rivers a nearby feature which is often overlooked is the adjoining meadows that lie in the alluvial flood plain. At first glance these marshy-looking fields, transected by numerous dykes and ditches, do not look particularly rewarding places to investigate. But until this century many of them had long histories of sympathetic management that ensured their productivity and created an environment where a great variety of plants and animals could live. Today, however, this continuity has been largely broken and many of these watermeadows have disappeared or are under threat. In lowland Britain those that remain represent some of our richest grassland habitats. So, in order to find out more we asked Dr Francis Rose, formerly Reader in Biogeography at King's College, London, now retired, and the author of many books on plants, to explore with us a typical watermeadow. On a lovely day in early July Francis took us to a quiet stretch of river in a beautiful corner of Hampshire. As we tramped down the curving path to the river he told us that the owner appreciated the need to preserve this very special habitat and that it has been designated as a Special Site of Scientific Interest. The owner consults with representatives of the Nature Conservancy Council in order to manage the meadows in the best possible way.

Dressed practically for the day and wearing our Wellingtons, we crossed the shallow, swiftly-flowing river by means of a plank bridge. From there we could see the river winding away into the distance around the area we had come to look at – a series of ancient watermeadows. Behind us, and further up the hill, fields were being worked with tractors and machines in the most modern way, a striking contrast to the tussocky land, seemingly dominated by rushes and sedges, which we now saw before us.

Francis first took us to an area that was slightly flatter than the rest and pointed out the carpet of exquisite orchids that surrounded us. Their pinks and purples stood out against a backcloth of greens. But before we looked at the plants in detail we asked him to tell us a little about the history of these places.

'Watermeadows are of special interest because of their exceptionally rich flora, a result of their very long histories and high levels of fertility due to regular flooding over many, many years.

'In previous centuries true watermeadows were carefully managed with a system of dykes, channels and ditches. In some cases a series of parallel ditches were cut across the meadow, the water levels being controlled by sluices. In the winter the water was allowed to flood onto the meadow through these ditches and to spread out on either side. When spring came the water was kept on the meadow for a time and then run off. This type of management is now very rare and can only be seen in a few places in the Avon Valley, Hampshire, and in Dorset.

'The type of meadow we are standing in today is, by comparison, much more common. There is no evidence that there were ever parallel ditches here. It is simply flooded by the river in winter, the silt enriching the soil with lime and other salts. Many of them were "laid up" for hay between March and July and after cutting were grazed by cattle and sheep. This site is too rough for hay so it is used primarily for grazing cattle.

'In the old days watermeadows were much sought after and, because of this, they were often shared. A few fascinating examples still remain. Near Cricklade, by the River Thames in Wiltshire, there is a series of old

A lovely specimen of one of our rarest meadow plants – the snake's head fritillary, *Fritillaria meleagris*. This flower used to have a much wider distribution along our lowland river valleys but it is now confined to a few sites particularly in the upper Thames Valley. Its decline parallels the change in agricultural practice as regards the use of the alluvial meadows, most of which have now been drained or reseeded. Its strange appearance is echoed in the many local names that it has acquired: 'dead men's bells' in Shropshire; 'lepers' lilies' in the west country, and 'toads' heads' in Wiltshire. It flowers early in spring before the taller plants have shaded it out.

watermeadows which is managed in the traditional way by lots. After the land has been cut for hay in mid-summer it becomes the common pasture of the Borough. From a natural history point of view this is of great benefit as, with several people involved, it is more difficult for anyone to decide to enclose or plough the meadows. This, however, is the exception, for in most parts of the country today watermeadows are treated as second-rate agricultural land. There is continuous pressure on these old meadows from farmers who want to "improve" them either by drainage and ploughing or conversion to ley pasture, often encouraged by government grants.

'The watermeadows we have visited today have a very rich flora and in this particular series of 200 to 300 acres well over 200 species of plants have been recorded. In the past there must have been many such sites, but now it is more common to find re-seeded pasture which often has a very low diversity of species, consisting sometimes of just rye grass and dutch clover. Apart from all of that, many of these meadows, particularly those in reach of large urban areas, have been quarried away for gravel pits.

'So it is nice to see what the old type of agricultural land was like and also to see how it created a habitat for a great diversity of plants and insects, for, if you have a great number of plants, you will also have a correspondingly large number of insects dependent on them. Here there are many butterflies and moths – the caterpillars feed on some of the plants – and dragonflies in turn feeding on other insects.

'A lot of these watermeadows probably have a pedigree going back thousands of years in one form of management or another. You never get quite the same set of species of plants and insects at any two sites. However, there is a common background of species that is found in all of them, each site having a certain individuality, which is something that one is very anxious to preserve.'

We asked Francis how we could recognise an old watermeadow. What were some of the features that marked it out from modern re-seeded pasture?

'First of all, there will be an obvious diversity of species. Even if one doesn't know what the species are, one can see that there are very many kinds of plant present. Secondly, the meadow will have a very

Opposite above **A secluded patch of meadow in full flower with the purple spikes of orchids contrasting with the whites and creams of the bedstraws and meadowsweet in the background.**

colourful appearance. On ancient grassland, particularly in June and July, one will see the pink or purple spikes of orchids. The modern leys don't usually have flowers in them, except perhaps white or red clover. Also in an old watermeadow one will see the rather quaintly shaped spikes of various sorts of sedges. In the more calcareous areas totter grass or quaking grass will be there with its very characteristic panicles and there may well be marsh horsetail with its strange pointed stems with little cones on top. That plant would not be found in a modern highly organised ley pasture. It is rough and harsh, and animals do not like eating it, so farmers won't have it around.

'So old communities of this kind tend to survive where the original types of management are still, for one reason or another, maintained. The farmer may be old-fashioned or he may be conservation-minded and feel that he can afford to manage some of his land in this way. One can argue that this type of herbage is really very much better for animals to eat because of its diversity. If you watch animals grazing on recently sown ley pasture and there is some more varied traditional grassland nearby, the animals will go and graze on that. Sometimes they'll graze along a hedge. Although it can be shown that they put on more weight if they are fed on certain types of modern ley pastures, the health of the animals, it is sometimes argued, is not necessarily better. Where there is a variety of species you tend to get more trace elements and more nutrient substances in the diet which may be important in ways which we don't yet fully understand.'

Having talked about some of the general aspects of these meadows and hinted at all their treasures, we were eager to explore them further. The most eye-catching plants around us were the tall spikes of the orchids. Francis went over to a nearby group and having inspected a few told us about them.

'We are now in an area of the watermeadow that is a bit lower than the rest. It is rather more damp and with a certain amount of grazing pressure which helps to keep out the really coarse vegetation, but not enough to suppress many of the flowering plants. Just here we can look across and see many different types of orchid in flower. Perhaps the most striking is the marsh fragrant orchid, *Gymnadenia densiflora*. There is a nice patch of them here. The common

fragrant orchid, *Gymnadenia conopsea*, is present on what are probably some of the drier hummocks. One can tell the difference between these two types of orchid in several ways: the common fragrant orchid flowers in June with paler rosy pink flowers and the side sepals are pointed and bend downwards. It has a pleasant sweet scent, but with a slightly rancid overtone. The marsh fragrant orchid, on the other hand, which usually prefers damper sites such as this, flowers a little later in the year with deeply coloured pinkish-purple flowers, and the square-ended sepals are spread out at right angles. It has a rich carnation scent.

'Besides the fragrant orchids, which are so abundant here they are adding a colourful hue to the overall scene, we have the commonest of our marsh orchids – the southern marsh orchid, *Dactylorhiza praetermissa*. It is still in flower although many of the individual plants are over now. The leaves of this handsome plant are unspotted and the rich purple and pink flowering spikes can be over a foot tall. I can see some common spotted orchids, *D. fuchsii*, which has similar, but pale pink, flowers and leaves which are heavily blotched and spotted. Growing on some *Sphagnum* moss over here is a more acid-loving relative – the heath

Two hoverflies feeding on the flowers of meadowsweet, *Filipendula ulmaria*, **one of the most well-known meadow plants.**

Opposite **Three flowering spikes of the dense-flowered or marsh fragrant orchid** *Gymnadenia densiflora*. **This orchid prefers damper habitats than the common fragrant orchid** *G. conopsea*. **It also has a more deeply coloured flower and a rich carnation scent.**

Left **The most typical orchid of base-rich fens and wet meadows is the southern marsh orchid** *Dactylorhiza praetermissa*, **which has a handsome spike of rich purple flowers and unspotted leaves.**

spotted orchid, *D. maculata*. These are rather similar to *D. fuchsii* but the lower lip of the flower is less three-lobed and more triangular with a distinct loop-like pattern as opposed to spots. However, it is a potentially confusing group of orchids as not only are there often distinct colour varieties but the different species frequently hybridize. Sometimes you find a colony where it is difficult to locate a pure specimen of any species. If we had been here earlier in the year we would have found another member of the *Dactylorhiza*, the early marsh orchid, *D. incarnata*.

'Some of the more common orchids, such as the spotted orchid, produce flower spikes for several years in succession, while others, like the burnt tip orchid, *Orchis ustulata*, flower once then lie dormant for years. This can result in fluctuations in the number of flowers that appear each year. Orchids are of great interest to a large number of people, not only because of their spectacular flowers, but also because of the many interesting aspects of their biology.'

We then moved on to a more bumpy area of the watermeadow where walking was rather difficult, so prominent were the hummocks

The large hummocks in the water meadow provided an interesting example of the soil preferences of certain plants. This hummock although standing on an alkaline soil had been leached at the top and had the acid-loving tormentil, *Potentilla erecta*, growing in its crown. Lower down, where the conditions were more basic, a marsh fragrant orchid had taken root.

above the bed of the meadow. Francis went on to describe the area.

'When we look at the ground more closely, we find that it is much more interesting than it first appears. The tops of the hummocks are raised above the chalky water for most of the year, perhaps even in winter, except in times of severe flood, and are obviously somewhat leached as a result. This is reflected in the variation in the plant life found in different parts of the hummocks.

'The soil on the tops is presumably more acid than in the lower parts and in the ground in between. So on top you find a few typical heathland plants such as tormentil, *Potentilla erecta*, with its bright yellow flowers. There is even the occasional bush of heather, *Calluna vulgaris*. Also, some of the tall tufts are dominated by clumps of the tussocky purple moor-grass, *Molinia caerulea*, which flowers later in the year. This is a grass one would normally associate with damp acid heathland.

'Even the different requirements of some of the plants are accommodated, as the tormentil and purple moor-grass, which prefer acid soils, are shallow rooted, while the fragrant orchid, which is sticking out of

the top here, is rooted down below in the calcareous soil beneath.

'This plant growing on the side is meadow vetchling, *Lathyrus pratensis*, one of the pea family. It is common on roadsides and here we can see it growing successfully on the well-drained hummock, rather than in the wetter spaces in between. Lower down we have some bog pimpernel, *Anagallis tenella*, which prefers damper more open conditions. Despite its name this plant is not restricted to bogs and can be found in marshes and mires ranging from very alkaline to weakly acid. It avoids the most acid bogs. For example, in the New Forest where some of the bogs are very acid you do find the bog pimpernel, but only in runnels of moving water where the pH is higher – above about 5·0. It has a charming little five-petalled flower which appears rosy pink. However, if you look closely you will find that the flowers are white with crimson veins. Another interesting point about the bog pimpernel is that, as you can see here, it is actually growing from a cushion of moss. This acts like a sponge in the wetter spells and retains its water when conditions are drier, keeping the shallow roots of the pimpernel moist.

'At the lowest level between the hummock and the floor of the meadow the soil is very chalky and we can find a number of plants typical of chalk grassland such as quaking grass, *Briza media*, and downy oat-grass, *Helictrotrichon pubescens*.

'If you look around there are a few more plants that one might expect to find on old downland turf. For instance we have some bird's-foot trefoil, *Lotus corniculatus*, and eyebright, *Euphrasia nemorosa*. In fact, this site has more in common with chalk down-land than one would think, being alkaline and also very much a product, in its present form, of human management. It is probable that there would have been swampy alder carr over much of this land at one time. This poses the interesting question: where were these plants, that we can see today, before man cut down the woods? I think the most likely view is that in earlier times the rivers were more unstable and frequently changed course, constantly producing new areas of marshland and other open habitats. Also we should not forget that in prehistoric times there were a large number of big herbivores in the countryside. These animals must have had an effect on our forests and river valleys. For example, you might have found aurochs grazing here at one time. If one thinks

A sedge and two rushes of fens and wet meadows: a) common sedge, *Carex nigra;* **b) soft rush,** *Juncus effusus;* **c) jointed rush,** *Juncus articulatus.*

further back, large numbers of bison and deer would be found and during the inter-glacial periods it has been discovered that hippos and rhinos were living in southern England. So in a sense when man came along with his domestic cattle and sheep he was merely replacing one form of grazing animal with another. However, one has to accept that during prehistoric times the amount of open habitat was far less than we have today. So it is regular grazing or mowing that has maintained the very diverse carpet of many small species of plant that we can see here. Without this, ranker species would soon increase, eventually pushing out the smaller plants. I think that this is an important point to remember if one wishes to conserve a site such as this. Even if you can get the co-operation of the owner or are able to pur-chase a site through the NCC or a local trust, just putting up a fence to keep everybody out is not good enough. This attitude is quite wrong because as we have seen the com-munity is dependent upon sympathetic management. Nearly every habitat in Britain has been created by the presence of some form of intervention by man, such as tradi-tional agricultural practice, and the survival

of the habitat depends on a continuity of this management. Just removing the grazing will eventually have almost as great an effect on the plant composition as actually ploughing it up. This is something which is not always sufficiently understood.'

As we walked around it was obvious that the sedges and rushes formed an important part of the rich plant community. We asked Francis to tell us some more about these superficially confusing groups.

'Sedges although apparently grass-like have solid triangular stems and have leaves in three vertical ranks. In the true sedges, *Carex*, the flowers are often grouped into a catkin-like male spikelet and several female spikelets. When there is a simple terminal spike the male flowers are found above the female. Sometimes male and female flowers are mixed in each spikelet.

'There are twenty different kinds of sedge in this area, forming quite a bulk of the herbage. Just here is an interesting one, the flea sedge, *Carex pulicaris*. This species has a single spike of flowers and the fruits that develop from the lower female flowers are about the same size and colours as fleas. Furthermore, if you gently brush them when

Above **The exquisite little flower of bog pimpernel,** *Anagallis tenella*. **This plant of damp meadows and marshes appears pink from a distance but when viewed this closely can be seen to be white with pink veins.**

Right **The ragged robin,** *Lychnis flos-cuculi*, **is a widespread member of the campion family that can grow in profusion in wet meadows. Plants with robin in their name are often associated with goblins – it is considered unlucky to pick this plant.**

they are ripe, the slight pressure causes them to jump off the spike rather in the way that a flea would.

'Here is an example of a sedge that has a terminal spike of male flowers and two or three female catkins below. This is black sedge, *Carex nigra*. The little green fruits lie behind black scales, called glumes, at this time of the year. Here is another – tawny sedge, *Carex hostiana*, which has more oval spikelets and more rounded fruits with long beaks. Another very local and interesting species can be seen over here – lesser panicled sedge, *Carex diandra*, in which all

the spikelets of the dense oblong flower-head have both male and female flowers although the female ones are below the males in each little spikelet, producing little brown fruits. That's a nice sedge to find in our meadow – dioecious sedge, *Carex dioica* This type of sedge has completely separate male and female plants. The female one has small triangular pointed fruits in an oval-shaped catkin at the top of the stem, while the male plant has a small cigar-shaped catkin of male flowers. This sedge seems to depend upon fairly wet conditions and short vegetation and is a plant that is very much at risk.

'Many of the rushes are of interest as well. This group of plants are thought to be descended from the lilies which are insect-pollinated and have accordingly attractive flowers. Rushes have gone over to wind pollination and therefore, in the course of evolution, their flowers have become reduced while the stigmas have increased in size and become feathery and sticky, more readily trapping the pollen which has become more copious and dusty so it is more easily carried along by the wind. The six petals are now no more than brown scales which merely protect the bud. Sedges and

One of the first flowers to bloom in marshes and damp meadows in early spring is the kingcup or marsh marigold, *Caltha palustris*. Its large leaves and clusters of giant buttercup-like flowers make it unmistakeable.

A great bank of meadowsweet or 'queen of the meadows'. This sweet smelling plant grows profusely in fens and wet meadows and in less sanitary days was used as a strewing herb on the floors of cottages.

grasses have gone even further in their specialised evolution towards wind pollination and have lost their petals altogether – only scale-like glumes enclose the florets.

'In this type of habitat we have two main types of rushes: those that have a terminal, branched flower-head and leaves that are jointed inside; and those that have no leaves, a spongy pith inside the stems and a lateral flower-head. There are about three species of each type here. For instance, this is the jointed rush, *Juncus articulatus*, in which, if you carefully split the leaf open with your thumb-nail, you can see the cross-partitions inside the leaf. There is a little spray of flowers at the top of the stem where you can see six pointed, brown petals, three little pink stigmas and three stamens in each flower. Another of the jointed rushes here is the blunt-flowered rush, *Juncus subnodulosus*. The flower is a much paler buff colour with little scale-like blunt petals. The fruit is also blunt but one can always identify this rush, even if it is not in fruit or flower, by simply opening a section of leaf where one will find that not only are there cross-partitions but also vertical ones.

'Here we have two species of the other type of rush – the hard rush, *Juncus inflexus*, and the soft rush, *J. effusus*. They both have their flower-heads seemingly coming out from the side of the stem but in fact, what looks like the upper part of the stem, above the flowers, is actually a bract. The hard rush is greyish-green in colour and the stem is strongly ribbed while the soft rush has a relatively smooth stem. Both have the spongy interior pith. These rushes are very typical of these wet meadows and fens.

'If we look around now, we should find some more flowering plants. Here is a very characteristic species – ragged robin, *Lychnis flos-cuculi*. This is a relative of the familiar red campion of hedgebanks and woods but has these petals that are very deeply divided into almost strap-like forks. The delicate flowers tend to flutter in the wind like little flags. Here is the meadow buttercup, *Ranunculus acris*. It is not too common here but on some meadows can become very abundant, which causes a problem for the farmer as it is poisonous, and instinctively avoided by grazing animals. Therefore, if it forms a large part of the herbage the farmer will be tempted to plough up the meadow and reseed it. If he does that his seed will almost certainly include these flowers here – red clover, *Trifolium pratense*, and white or

dutch clover, *T. repens*. They are able to fix the nitrogen in the soil through their root nodules and therefore contribute to the overall productivity of the meadow.

'It is worth mentioning that in this diverse habitat you can find some species that are more typically found in damp woodlands. For instance, here we have the large leaves of marsh marigold or kingcup, *Caltha palustris*, whose large showy yellow flowers are long since over. Another plant that falls into this category is wild angelica, *Angelica sylvestris*.

'This little patch of fairly open meadow shows us two species that underline the nature of the pedigree of this site. First, we have an increasingly local plant, the meadow thistle, *Cirsium dissectum*. This is a plant that most people might not recognise as a thistle, because it has very feeble little prickles on the edge of an almost undivided leaf. In fact, it looks more like a knapweed. Growing next to these is a little colony of yellow rattles, *Rhinanthus minor*. This little member of the figwort family has typical yellow, two-lipped figwort flowers with a purple spotted stem and narrow pairs of leaves. It has a very inflated calyx shaped like a little pouch flattened on either side. When the seeds are ripe they rattle about inside the calyx. Like the meadow thistle, it is a plant of old meadows but unlike it, it does not seem to have a preference as to whether the soil is wet or dry, as long as it is moderately alkaline. This plant is, in fact, a semi-parasite and, although it has green leaves and can manufacture its own food, to flower successfully it needs to make a connection with one of the meadow grasses.'

As we crossed over to a wetter area of the meadow, Francis pointed out some of the commoner species of grass that were present: Yorkshire fog, *Holcus lanatus*; red fescue-grass, *Festuca rubra*, and some sweet vernal grass, *Anthoxanthum odoratum*. The vegetation gradually was becoming taller with little wet hollows that were bursting with mosses. We now started to encounter one of the most well-known of the watermeadow plants – meadowsweet, *Filipendula ulmaria*. Francis pointed out that it was also called the 'queen of the meadows'. And rightly so as the tall flower-heads were producing an almost solid mass of creamy-white. The scent that they were giving off was very sweet. This area was probably less often grazed by the cattle and that combined with the wetter regime meant that we were to find some new plants. One of the most noticeable was the

Above **The flowering spike of the marsh helleborine,** *Epipactis palustris.* **This charming member of the orchid family is a local plant of fens and meadows.**

Right **The tip of a marsh lousewort or red rattle,** *Pedicularis palustris,* **showing the fern-like leaves and the reddish-pink flower.**

Opposite **A yellow flag,** *Iris pseudacorus,* **with sunlit water behind. This is a plant of marshes and damper areas where the water table is permanently high.**

bogbean, *Menyanthes trifoliata*, with its large trefoil leaves. Francis told us some more about it and also pointed out some plants of interest.

'At this time of year we can see the seed capsules of the bogbean. They are quite large and each contains a number of little egg-like seeds, three or four millimetres long. If we had come earlier in the year, we would have seen its beautiful white, five-petalled flowers. They are fringed like the edge of a piece of Turkish towelling.

'Here we have the leaves of a rather nice member of the parsley or umbellifer family – pepper saxifrage, *Silaum silaus*. It is very characteristic of ancient meadows and is certainly decreasing. It has longer, more narrow and linear segments to its leaves than cow parsley. In August when it flowers you will see that it has bright sulphur yellow umbels of flowers. The name comes from the fruits that have a peppery smell, if you crush them. Another tall perennial plant of these wetter areas that we are fortunate to have here is the common meadow-rue, *Thalictrum flavum*. This is becoming quite a rarity these

A view of the dense
growth of the wetter
areas in the water
meadow with the tall
growth of marsh
thistle, *Cirsium palustre*,
in the centre. Habitat
like this is extremely
rich in plant species.

days, although according to Victorian botanists it was relatively common. Again the
chief reason for its disappearance is the
destruction of old meadows and the general
tidying up of river banks. It has a spray of
rather pretty flowers without any petals; it is
the stamens that are the conspicuous part of
the flower. It has compound leaves with
rather narrow wedge-shaped leaflets. It used
to be particularly fond of the banks of the
channels which fed the water onto the
meadow in the winter. To give you an idea of
how scarce it is becoming, I know myself of
only one other site in Hampshire where it is
to be found today.

'Looking now at some of the mossy
depressions in between the taller plants, we
have a couple of rather nice plants. The first
one is another member of the figwort family –
red rattle or marsh lousewort, *Pedicularis
palustris*. It has these rather attractive highly
divided fern-like leaves and a reddish-purple
tube-like flower with a prominent lower lip.
The calyx, like its cousin the yellow rattle, is
inflated. This lovely plant is now extinct in
Sussex and Kent, due to drainage. Growing
next to it is another plant typical of these
places – the marsh helleborine, *Epipactis
palustris*. This orchid is very characteristic of
fenland but will also occur in old meadow
systems where there are deeper hollows with
more permanent high water tables. They are
rather distinctive in appearance in that
unlike other orchids the leaves are elliptical
and pointed with strong veins and are along
the stem rather than in a rosette at its base.
The flower spike is rather loose with ten to
fifteen flowers. Each flower has a most
beautiful white lip with a yellow spot in the
centre. The frilly edge to this gives it the
appearance of a cravat of an eighteenth
century clergyman in miniature. There are
three spreading sepals which are a delicate
purplish-grey on the outside and a more
pinky-white on the inside. This orchid is
pollinated entirely by honey bees. Unfortunately, it is far scarcer than it used to be,
due to the drainage of suitable habitats.

'We are quite close to a stream and
standing up conspicuously in front of us are
some yellow iris, *Iris pseudocorus*, with the
leaves characteristically all arranged in one
plane. The familiar yellow flower is adding a
splash of colour to this part of the meadows,
but this plant really indicates that we are now
in fen country and if we look just a little way
ahead we can see the enormous tussocks of
the greater panicled sedge, *Carex paniculata*,

fringing the steam. The general abundance of the bogbean just here also confirms the permanently wet conditions. So I suggest we head across to a dryer section.'

We made our way carefully through the tall ranks of flag, being careful not to trample any of the delicate plants. Soon we were walking over very different ground as a series of drier ridges across the meadows provided us with a glimpse of classic chalk grassland complete with magnificent anthills garlanded in thyme and squinancywort. The whole scene was a most unexpected and fascinating delight. As Francis picked his way between the anthills pointing out some of the typical chalk downland plants, a green woodpecker suddenly took off in front of us letting out its distinctive laughing cry It disappeared into some nearby scrub, which was standing like Birnam Wood about to move on Dunsinane. Francis took up the story.

'If the grazing pressure was reduced or stopped the hawthorn scrub, particularly in these drier ridges, would rapidly invade the grassland which, in turn, would mean that scrub would also encroach on the wetter areas. So that willow and alder carr could take over larger areas until, theoretically, the whole series of watermeadows would disappear under a climax of oak woodland. So the balance of these places is extremely precarious. Something which must always be borne in mind when studying these sites and proposing any management plans.'

The afternoon was coming to an end, so we made our way back across the meadows trying on the one hand not to tread on any of the orchids and on the other not to fall over the hummocks. Whilst tackling this rather unusual problem we happened to flush up a snipe. As we watched it fly in a frenzied zig-zag path away from us, Francis pointed out how important these relatively undisturbed areas of roughly grazed meadow were for nesting snipe and redshank. Indeed, if the plant communities have been suffering from the loss of this habitat, the decline of the breeding populations of these birds in lowland Britain has been equally as dramatic.

As we walked back over the river and up the hill to the cars we realised that we would now look at watermeadows with their rich patchwork of flowers in a very different light. It was comforting to know that these, at least, would have a continuity of management that hopefully would ensure they were looked after for future generations to discover afresh.

Further reading

Bang, P. and Dahlstrom, P., *Animal Tracks and Signs*, Collins (1974).

Bellamy, D. J., *Bellamy on Botany*, BBC Publications (1972, revised 1975).

Bellamy, D. J., *Bellamy's Britain*, BBC Publications (1974).

Bellamy, D. J., *Botanic Man*, Hamlyn (1978).

Brown, R. W. and Lawrence, M. J., *Mammals of Britain*, Blandford (1967, revised 1974).

Bruun, B. and Singer, A., *The Hamlyn Guide to Birds of Britain and Europe*, Hamlyn (1970, revised 1978).

Chinery, M., *A Field Guide to the Insects of Britain and Northern Europe*, Collins (1973).

Clarke, P. *et al*, *The Sunday Times 1000 Days Out in Great Britain and Ireland*, Macdonald (1981).

Corbet, G. B. and Southern, H. N. (eds.), *The Handbook of British Mammals*, Blackwell (1977).

Darlington, A., *The Pocket Encyclopaedia of Plant Galls*, Blandford (1968, revised 1975).

Holliday, F. G. T., *Wildlife of Scotland*, Macmillan (1979).

Hubbard, C. E., *Grasses*, Penguin (1968).

Humphries, C. J., Press, J. R., Sutton, D. A., *The Hamlyn Guide to Trees of Britain and Europe*, Hamlyn (1981).

Lousley, J. E., *Wild Flowers of Chalk and Limestone*, Collins (rev. ed. 1969).

Mabey, R., *The Common Ground*, Arrow (1981).

Measures, D., *Bright Wings of Summer*, Cassell (1977).

Morris, P. (ed.), *The Natural History of the British Isles*, Country Life (1979).

Phillips, R., *Grasses, Ferns, Mosses and Lichens of Great Britain and Ireland*, Pan (1980).

Pollard, E., Hooper, M. D. and Moore, N. W., *Hedges*, Collins (1974).

Rose, F., *Wildflower Key*, Warne (1981).

Whalley, P., *Butterfly Watching*, Severn House (1980).

Organisations to join

Botanical Society of the British Isles
68 Outwoods Road, Loughborough, Leicestershire.
A national society for both amateur and professional botanists. Organises mapping schemes and is active in the conservation of our wild plants.

British Butterfly Conservation Society
Tudor House, Quorn, Leicester.

British Trust for Conservation Volunteers
10–14 Duke Street, Reading, Berkshire RG1 4RU.
An organisation for people over sixteen years of age which undertakes practical projects, such as clearing scrub, maintaining reserves, tree-planting, etc.

British Trust for Ornithology
Beech Grove, Tring, Hertfordshire.
National organisation which carries out research into all aspects of bird life supported by a growing army of amateur enthusiasts.

Ramblers' Association
1–5 Wandsworth Road, London SW8 2LJ.

Royal Society for Nature Conservation
The Green, Nettleham, Lincoln.
The Royal Society for Nature Conservation is the national association of the 44 local Nature Conservation Trusts which form the major voluntary organisation concerned with all aspects of wildlife conservation in the United Kingdom. The Trusts have a combined membership of 140,000 and, together with the Society, own or manage over 1,300 nature reserves throughout the UK covering a range of sites, from woodland and heathland to wetland and estuarine habitats. Most Trusts have full-time staff but the members themselves, with a wide range of skills, contribute greatly to all aspects of the work.

Royal Society for the Protection of Birds
The Lodge, Sandy, Bedfordshire.
The major conservation organisation for birds and their habitats.

The Scottish Wildlife Trust
25 Johnston Terrace, Edinburgh EH1 2NH.
The Scottish branch of the County Conservation Trusts.

Watch: The Watch Trust for Environmental Education
22 The Green, Nettleham, Lincoln LN2 2NR.
Sponsored by *The Sunday Times* and the *Royal Society for Nature Conservation;* WATCH is a national club for children and young teenagers.

Index

Figures in italics refer to illustrations